BRITISH PSYCHOLOGY IN CRISIS

BRITISH PSYCHOLOGY IN CRISIS

A Case Study in Organisational Dysfunction

Edited by

David Pilgrim

PHOENIX
PUBLISHING HOUSE
firing the mind

First published in 2023 by
Phoenix Publishing House Ltd
62 Bucknell Road
Bicester
Oxfordshire OX26 2DS

British Library Cataloguing in Publication Data

A C.I.P. for this book is available from the British Library

ISBN-13: 978-1-80013-184-2

Typeset by Medlar Publishing Solutions Pvt Ltd, India

www.firingthemind.com

Contents

About the editor and contributors

Graham Buchanan is a writer, educator, and advisor specialising in all aspects of strategy and leadership. From 2003 to 2015, he was a director of studies at the Leadership Academy for Policing with national responsibility for community engagement, media strategy, and finance. From 2013 to 2019, he was a visiting professor at London Guildhall Faculty of Business and Law, part of London Metropolitan University, where he was patron of the master's programme in strategic management and leadership. He is a chartered fellow of the Chartered Management Institute, and a fellow of the Royal Society of Arts. He has developed the innovative 'Eleven Hats of Leadership'.

Ashley Conway is a counselling psychologist who has worked with clients with severe trauma for over twenty-five years. He has a special interest in memory of trauma, particularly of childhood abuse. He is a co-editor of and contributor to the international award-winning book *Trauma and Memory: The Science and the Silenced*. He is currently chair of the charity CDS-UK (Clinic for Dissociative Studies), which helps provide education in the field and therapy for clients suffering severe dissociative problems, which can emerge as a result of prolonged childhood trauma.

Pat Harvey was an NHS clinical psychologist for over thirty years, managing a large psychology and counselling service. She helped set up the Lancashire training scheme for clinical psychologists, taught professional issues on the course, and was an examiner for the BPS Diploma. She served as a Mental Health Act Commissioner from 1983 to 1986, and was elected and served as chair of the BPS Division of Clinical Psychology 1997–1998. After retiring in 2002, she left psychology and obtained a master's degree in fine art printmaking and practised as a visual artist. Having retained BPS membership, she joined with others in 2020 to question the organisational and policy directions of the Society and runs the critical commentary Twitter account @psychsocwatchuk.

David Pilgrim has a background in both psychology and sociology. Now semi-retired, he is visiting professor of clinical psychology at the University of Southampton and honorary professor of health and social policy at the University of Liverpool. His publications include *Understanding Mental Health: A Critical Realist Exploration* (Routledge, 2015) and *Key Concepts in Mental Health* (fifth edition, Sage, 2019). Others include *A Sociology of Mental Health and Illness*, now in its sixth edition (Open University Press, 2005—winner of the 2006 BMA Medical Book of the Year Award), *Mental Health Policy in Britain* (Palgrave, 2002), and *Mental Health and Inequality* (Palgrave, 2003) (all with Anne Rogers). His most recent books are *Child Sexual Abuse: Moral Panic or State of Denial?* (Routledge, 2018), *Critical Realism for Psychologists* (Routledge, 2020), and *Identity Politics: Where Did It All Go Wrong?* (Phoenix, 2022).

Editor's preface

This book is a case study on organisational dysfunction. At the time of writing, there is much evidence that the British Psychological Society (BPS) is in crisis, as will become clear in the pages to come. 'Crisis' is an over-used word, and it may suggest a transitory period of acute disturbance, soon to pass. However, the problems in the BPS are neither temporary nor recent. They are longstanding, going back decades. They involve ingrained cultural norms of a poorly governed, opaque, and anti-democratic organisational structure.

At some point, these norms would inevitably culminate in corruption, which has been the case here. That corruption has involved both financial gain and the abuse of power. To date, the conditions of possibility for this outcome have not been dealt with honestly by its leadership, nor have they been reformed sufficiently to prevent a recurrence of the problems addressed in this book.

Although we focus on the structural fault at the centre of the BPS, which encourages a lack of transparency and prevents independent public scrutiny, those filling leadership roles have frequently capitalised on this fault, not sought to correct it. We are looking here at the ambiguous question of the relationship between structural determinants and the role of personal agency, in explaining the degree to which human organisations are commendable or condemnable.

Although the BPS is a charity, it is not run in the public interest and its Board of Trustees are not independent. Although the BPS is purportedly a scholarly organisation, it has failed to uphold some basic expectations of academic probity. It is fair to say that is neither a learned, nor a learning, organisation. More recently, censorship has become normalised by its managers and those controlling its published material. Propaganda and 'spin' from new managers-for-hire, with no loyalty to academic values, have sabotaged traditional expectations of freedom of expression.

Although the BPS is purportedly a membership organisation, it has been characterised by the poor involvement of ordinary members. The latter have often been kept in the dark about what is happening at the centre of the BPS, and when they have expressed their concerns, they have been ignored, palmed off, or sent into the long grass of an arcane complaints process. If they have complained 'too much' or too vociferously, in frustration (in the view of the Society's leadership), then they have been accused of harassing BPS staff.

Although the BPS offers the outside world the confident expectation of balanced and inclusive advice about public policy matters, its poor governance has created opportunities for policy capture. The latter has failed to represent the full gamut of evidence and debate about policy topics and, in doing so, at times this has placed the public at risk of harm.

Some elected as president for the Society have made genuine attempts to rectify the obdurate systemic problems of poor governance. Those efforts have met resistance, and the reformers have been punished, left frustrated, or been expelled because of the threat they have posed to the reactionary beneficiaries of mismanagement. Many presidents have made no such efforts, but simply been complicit in the norms of organisational dysfunction which they have encountered. The bottom line has been that individual presidents, whether reforming or complicit, have made little or no difference to the ingrained dysfunction that has now become an existential threat to the BPS.

The BPS is by no means an isolated example of a poorly governed organisation today. However, what makes it an unnerving example, for anyone new to it, is the fact that it is called a *Psychological* Society. This might raise the reasonable public expectation of an organisational culture characterised by honesty, rationality, and reflexivity. The public might, quite understandably, expect a particularly high standard of personal sensitivity and insight from such a named organisation. Sadly, to date, this has not been the case. If we have here an expectation of 'physician heal thyself', then we are still all waiting patiently for that promise to be fulfilled.

The organisational failures listed above are explored in the book, borne of the experience of those campaigning to reverse them. The authors are not nihilistic; all, bar one, are longstanding members of the BPS and genuinely look for evidence of remediation. They would like their criticisms to be taken seriously as a resource for corrective feedback, even though they are travelling more in hope than expectation. However, it may be that the rot in the organisation has gone too far.

A wider consideration is that single disciplines are no longer a credible source of authority to solve the challenges facing humanity in the twenty-first century, as the end of the Anthropocene looms. Maybe claims of disciplinary imperialism, common in the twentieth century, are no longer fit for purpose today. The world is in particular need of interdisciplinary cooperation, in a spirit of humility and transparency, from its scholarly contributors. As will become evident in what is to come in the book, neither of these required features come easy to those seeking to preserve the status quo in the BPS.

CHAPTER 1

The history of the BPS crisis

David Pilgrim

This first chapter describes the current legitimation crisis in the British Psychological Society (BPS). For decades, the Society has been prone to many problems of poor governance. These have impaired its credibility as a learned body, which rhetorically claims a right to public confidence.[1] I start by outlining a description of the crisis for those new to it, before moving to its historical conditions of possibility:

1. In recent times, the BPS has lost one elected president after another, and some have tried and failed to correct the evident dysfunction they encountered after their election. In 2021, no fewer than three departed over a two-month period, with two resigning and one being expelled before their period of office was up. In August 2022, the president elect resigned before taking up her role, citing fears of pressures within the organisation that would impact adversely on her professional life.
2. In 2020, a major fraud came to light, implicating a former employee. In January 2022, she was sentenced to twenty-eight months in prison for defrauding the Society of over £70,000. She had been imprisoned

in the past for a similar offence in two other organisations (a total of seventeen offences). The BPS appointed her despite this past record, noted very publicly in the press. Since the turn of this century, other 'financial irregularities' in the Society have been dealt with by internal investigations and staff departures. The BPS membership has been kept in the dark about these events.

3. The Charity Commission[2] has 'engaged' with the Society about its broken complaints process and its lack of adequate governance. However, to date, this engagement has not ensured any observable organisational reform of substance. The Commission has received many expressions of concern from BPS members, and this pattern continues as the crisis fails to resolve. A particular challenge we face at present is that the Charity Commission itself has been ineffectual.

4. Whilst fair charges of misgovernance and corruption can be made about the BPS, these accusations have not been addressed publicly, or fairly and squarely, by the leadership of the Society. Instead, legitimate criticisms and queries have been ignored and denied.

5. For a year (between November 2020 and November 2021), the chief executive officer (CEO) of the Society, Sarb Bajwa, was suspended in the wake of the fraud investigation noted in (2) above. His finance director was also suspended at the same time (November 2020), but within a month, he left to take up a new position at the National Lottery Community Fund, while still under investigation. At the time of writing, he remains employed there.

6. Despite all of the above, the leadership of the Society has failed to keep its members[3] informed of the crisis. The BPS is allegedly a membership organisation, and good practice requires transparency and accountability from the Board of Trustees (BoT) and senior management team (SMT). They have clearly failed in that regard.

7. Some in this book have collaborated, since late 2020, in the formation of 'BPSWatch'[4] (more on this in Chapter 3). They are experienced psychologists and long-term members of the Society. Their efforts have been directed at exposing wrongdoing and negligence in the BPS.

8. This recent organisational turbulence reflects longstanding structural and cultural difficulties in the Society in recent decades.

The dysfunctional organisational dynamics are not new (see later), but they appear to have intensified more recently.

That final point is a cue to explore the history of the crisis and, for the new reader, the next section offers an account of those conditions of possibility.

A very brief history of British psychology

For at least 2,000 years, matters of the mind had fallen within the jurisdiction of philosophers and clerics. By the end of the nineteenth century, two professional responses were emerging in reaction to this pre-Enlightenment scenario. In Continental Europe, psychoanalytical ideas were beginning to influence the arts and humanities, and were shaping the beginnings of psychotherapy in clinical settings. This hermeneutic[5] approach to psychology competed with a second.

In Germany, Britain, and North America, empiricism and positivism were guiding that version of psychological science which sought to mimic physical science and experimentalism.[6] Its rationale for the emerging discipline was summed up here in the very first page of the first editorial of the *British Journal of Psychology* from James Ward and William Rivers:[7]

> Psychology, which till recently was known amongst us chiefly as mental philosophy and was widely concerned with problems of a more or less speculative and transcendental character, has now at length achieved the position of a *positive science*; one of a special interest to the philosopher no doubt but still *independent of his control*, possessing its *own methods*, its own specific problems and a distinct standpoint altogether its own. 'Ideas' in the philosophical sense *do not fall within its scope*; its inquiries are restricted entirely to *facts*. (emphasis added)

At the outset, the tiny group forming the BPS remained ambivalently attached to philosophy, reflecting the existing disciplinary allegiance of some of its members. For example, in 1902, one founding member and philosopher, George Stout, proposed that the new journal should be subsumed in the main philosophy journal *Mind*, but this was not supported by the rest.[8] Ward and Rivers were setting out the stall above then for a version of psychology which was to be both anti-psychoanalytical and anti-philosophical. For its first fifty years, the discipline was shaped by empiricism and positivism; even today, these resonate strongly in defining its legitimacy. I develop this point a little more now.

The complexities of process and content in the organisation of the discipline

Most of the organisational dysfunction we explore in this book about the BPS reflects processes present in many other bureaucracies and businesses. However, in learned bodies, which risk making authoritative claims about human experience and conduct, the disciplinary content is particularly relevant to its politics. The long-term credibility, or otherwise, of the declaration from Ward and Rivers today is uncertain, and this uncertainty exists beyond the organisational boundaries of the BPS.

As well as this contestation internally, about what should and should not constitute legitimate psychological knowledge, the discipline also has had the challenge of defining its authority relative to competitors close by, such as sociology, philosophy (which has not gone away), and anthropology. Distinguishing its authority from 'lay psychologies'[9] has also been an ongoing challenge for the discipline. It is still not always clear whether professional psychologists offer knowledge that is superior to common-sense understandings of human experience and conduct, or the explorations, for example, of good novelists.

That dilemma of boundary formation applied from the beginning of the BPS, which was formed in 1901, initially as the 'Psychological Society', by a small group of philosophers and medical practitioners.[10] They found that several small lay societies claiming the same name existed, so the prefix 'British' was agreed in 1906, to distinguish its scholarly authority from these minnows. Nonetheless, for many years, its jurisdiction in the academy was constrained by academic philosophers, with their traditional assumed authority over the mind. For example, by 1939, there were only six chairs of psychology in the British university system,[11] which reflected the brake being imposed by academic philosophy departments.

The stall set out by Ward and Rivers was empiricist and positivist, built on the legacy of Locke and Hume. It eschewed interpretation, speculation, and theory-building. However, as with any other academic discipline worth its salt, psychology *needed* theories. Empiricism tends to have a de-theorising impact when put into practice. In the case of Britain, imported reinvigorating theories were required, by and large.[12] Thus a contradiction was evident: by rejecting philosophy, but also mindlessly incorporating a *version* of it, the new empiricists in psychology weakened their own competence at pre-empirical and non-empirical reflection. (I return to this point in Chapter 10 and its implications for organisational amnesia in Britain.)

'Science', 'facts', and 'evidence' glowed proudly in the rhetoric of the new discipline. However, in the absence of philosophical competence, scientistic dogma, rather than philosophical clarity and depth, was offered to student and public audiences. Both empiricism and positivism in the philosophy of science were to be problematised increasingly during the twentieth century. However, these emerging metaphysical debates about the nature of scientific evidence were taught poorly, if at all, in academic departments of psychology. This is relevant today if students are to reflect at all, let alone intelligently, on the recurring crises in their discipline.[13]

This poor capacity for pre-empirical and non-empirical reflection was to have a bearing on how British psychology might then adapt, for over a century, to a range of competitors to naïve realism across the arts and humanities, and even in disputes about the philosophy of natural science. This absence of philosophical sophistication mattered in particular in the case of the emergent discipline of psychology. It existed, and still does, at the cusp of the biological and social sciences. Its legitimacy then rests upon a clear philosophical appreciation of the strengths and weaknesses of each, which would constitute a whole undergraduate curriculum in its own right.

These epistemological challenges in Britain also were complicated by the strong co-presence of psychoanalysis, international tensions about which were situated, by a quirk of history, in North London. The work of Karl Popper, a key émigré, critiqued *both* psychoanalysis *and* the naïve realism of Ward and Rivers. Instead, Popper favoured critical rationalism.[14] He noted that science was a value-inflected social activity, and so the naïve separation of facts from values (following Hume) to offer 'disinterested facts' (a favoured claim of positivists) was a false trail. Science is value-inflected, and empirical detachment is particularly challenging in human science (and wider social science), as we are part of the object of our inquiry. I return to this matter of the philosophy of science in Chapter 8.

In competition with this corrective of positivism from Popper in the 1960s, there emerged another philosophical challenge: the impact of postmodernism in the 1980s. The ultra-relativism and 'perspectivism' of the latter were derived from Nietzsche, who offered this stark contrast to the position of Ward and Rivers:

> Against those who say 'There are only facts,' I say, 'No, facts are precisely what there is not, only interpretations.' We cannot establish any fact in itself. Perhaps it is folly to want to do such a thing. Insofar as the word 'knowledge' has any meaning, the world is knowable; but it is interpretable otherwise. It has no meaning behind it, but countless meanings.[15]

This notion of 'countless meanings' created a challenge for empiricist psychology in Britain and practical problems for the BPS. How was the British discipline to retain a coherent persona, given these epistemological tensions? Having seemingly fended off the authority of psychoanalysis in Britain during the post-war period, for example from those like Hans Eysenck,[16] what was to be done now with postmodern relativism and radical social constructivism?

The fetish of empiricism had sacralised quantitative methods. Hume's insistence that facts are proven by the demonstration of observable 'constant conjunctions' gave confidence to the position of eugenic quantitative researchers (such as Karl Pearson, Charles Spearman, Cyril Burt, and Hans Eysenck).[17] I return to their problematic role in British psychology in Chapter 8.

Moreover, the closed system of the psychological laboratory was idealised. That setting allowed psychologists to *control* interfering variables that might cloud the facts borne of correlations between 'dependent' and 'independent' variables.[18] This meant *controlling out* the messy complexity of an open system in constant flux,[19] which was the real world inhabited by applied psychologists (and the general public). Extrapolating then from the closed system of the laboratory to unique biographies, embedded in the fluxing multiple social forces of an open system, became a precarious and sometimes preposterous exercise. Evidence for this point will be examined in particular in Chapter 5 by Ashley Conway.

But the problem of insensitivity to context, for the norms of empiricism and positivism declared by Ward and Rivers in 1904, was not the only one. With the postmodern turn of the 1980s, narratives and discourses became the focus and so *qualitative* methods (especially discourse analysis and deconstruction) became modish in Western psychology.[20] Squaring the circle of traditional naïve realism and postmodernism, with its affordance of identity politics and radical social constructivism, was a clear disciplinary challenge. The partisan role of identity politics in shaping policy capture in the BPS is discussed by Pat Harvey in Chapter 4.

The pragmatic solution for psychology (represented by bodies like the BPS) was to redefine its legitimacy not by theory but by method. Now those schooled in psychology in the academy, and especially those going on to research and teach the subject, shifted their rhetoric of justification from theory (say behaviourism or cognitivism) to methodology. 'Methodologism'[21] now began to characterise the discipline.

Colleagues in the corridor of a university psychology department might range from biologists to social psychologists, with their variegated theoretical preferences. However, what they could now all agree upon was the importance of methodological rigour. This tactic might now differentiate psychology from other disciplines, such as philosophy, sociology,[22] and anthropology (and, of course, the laity that had been so troublesome between 1901 and 1906). Whether that disciplinary distinction and claims of pre-eminence about matters psychological have been persuasive remains an open question.

Theory and practice

Returning to the development of the BPS during the twentieth century, it may have begun as an academic interest group, but the practical challenges and policy opportunities of being part of its host society were also apparent. The first Sections (Medical and Educational), which were formed in the Society shortly after the First World War, began to reflect this point. The 'Great War', like the one being stored up for twenty years hence, afforded both obligations and opportunities for the Society. This scenario witnessed the weaving together of the contradictory elements of eugenics (noted above from University College London) and psychoanalysis (from medical psychotherapists, via the Tavistock Clinic).

After the Second World War in the BPS, new sub-systems, and its membership, expanded, with an increasing separation of Divisions from Sections. The former represented those with postgraduate qualifications in an applied area (such as clinical, educational, or occupational settings), leaving the Sections retained as academic interest groups. Together these then constituted a sub-system network in the BPS, which was overseen by overarching Boards. This structuring of the Society was to be influential in the way in which its leadership arrangements were to be constituted later. They became the sites for the expression of power and opposition to it, discussed at length in later chapters.

The period between 1950 and 1988 was one in which certain cultural features in the BPS were becoming obvious. First, the applied wing was becoming prestigious publicly, but the control of the inner workings of the Society was still exercised largely by academic psychologists.

Second, that separation was played out in different arenas of control. The elected presidential side of the organisation was being occupied increasingly by applied psychologists. The Divisional sub-systems developed their own identities and group loyalties, and would feel more or less supported by academics governing BPS Boards. On that Board side (with jurisdiction for research, testing, and teaching standards), the academics clearly held sway. The same senior names from both sides recurred year on year, setting the oligarchical trend to be discussed later in this book.

Third, the contradictions of the past about empiricism and psychodynamic ideas remained. For example, the Medical Section of the Society (the oldest sub-system) was under the continuing control of medical psychotherapists, many of whom were psychoanalysts. This led to a *putsch* for control in 1958 by clinical psychologists, who were methodological behaviourists working at the Institute of Psychiatry.[23] By 1963, the *Journal of Clinical Psychology* was set up as an alternative to the *Journal of Medical Psychology* (from the contested Medical Section). By 1966, a separate Division of Clinical Psychology then marked an emergent new professional identity.[24]

When we look now at the list of presidents during this period, increasingly the post-holders were applied, especially clinical, psychologists. This set the scene for political tensions at the centre. It is not surprising that a major sign of the BPS fragmenting was in 2017, with the formation of the Association of Clinical Psychologists (ACP). These 'defectors' from the parent body made it clear that this schism was the result of years of struggling with an arcane bureaucracy that, from their point of view, was unsupportive of, and insensitive to, the challenges of clinical practice.

The leaders of the breakaway were well seasoned in the workings of the Division of Clinical Psychology and other BPS sub-systems. They were not petulant youngsters, but frustrated and weary ageing BPS members. This was also the case with an earlier split-off by many in the Division of Occupational Psychology in 2000 to form the Association of Business Psychologists (ABP).[25] They too felt poorly served by membership of the BPS.

This fracturing reflected a clear crisis in the capacity of the BPS to contain old contradictions, when aspiring to reconcile pure and applied psychology. These inner tensions and the continuing need to restate the authority claimed by Ward and Rivers, despite the persistent irritant of psychodynamic ideas still in the system, were the cultural context for the period up until 1988. Eventually, postmodernism disrupted the norms of legitimacy in the discipline further. The culture of the BPS was inflected by other new factors as well, which I now address.

The missed opportunity of 1988

The above summary of tensions inside the BPS left it as an ambiguous organisation. It was not a trade union (say like the British Medical Association), but neither was it a clear-cut academic body, given that the concerns of so many of its members were about daily practice in non-academic settings. Also, membership eligibility was determined by being a psychology graduate but, other than that, its members may have had little in common. At one end of the spectrum were academics and practitioners who lived and breathed psychology, but even then in markedly different settings. At the other were members who were little concerned in their daily lives with matters psychological.

This was the state of play by the 1980s, when two cultural shifts began to be influential. The first, already mentioned, was the postmodern turn and the compromises about 'methodologism' which this necessitated. The second was about the emergence of the new public management (NPM)[26] model arising from the hegemonic period of Margaret Thatcher's premiership during the 1980s.

Across the public and charity sectors there was a move from administration to management. Professionalisation was now not only about the discipline of psychology (reflected in the extant Divisional system), but also *the organisation that represented it, the BPS*. This was the new context for the most recent crisis in the Society, described at the start of this chapter. Two cultural trends were relevant in the Thatcher period. First, matters of business efficiency, value for money, and public reputation came together. Psychologists began to 'power-dress' and embrace managerialism. Moreover, they pushed for formal chartering arrangements (an initiative driven successfully by the Division of Clinical Psychology).

Second, the establishment of a modified Royal Charter for the Society in 1988 allowed senior managers of the Society to celebrate a new dawn. It was an organisation (just like the case of the NHS) which was to be managed, not merely administered, and it was to hold its own register of psychologists. This was announced with the hyperbole, typical of the times, with this statement from the executive secretary of the Society, Colin Newman:

> as in the theory of evolution, cataclysmic events occur which result in more dramatic, sudden revolutionary changes ... One such cataclysmic event has just occurred in the national environment in which the Society exists. In 1987, the Privy Council granted the order in Council[27] amending the Royal Charter and Statutes of the Society, thereby authorizing the Society to maintain a Register of Chartered Psychologists.[28]

This bombast was to be a short-lived, and so hollow, celebration of being a registration body (see later).

More importantly, the 1988 revision of the Royal Charter defining this charitable body required that it set up a BoT. This was an opportunity to create a *truly independent* BoT and shift from the flawed model adopted in the original Royal Charter of the Society in 1965.[29] Even by the 1980s, there was a growing sensibility that charities should have proper external scrutiny to ensure probity, and the 1965 model was not fit for purpose.

The 1965 version remained in place in 1988 and is still there today, though very recently minor revisions have been made to incorporate outsider scrutiny. The BoT has had no independent trustees[30] but instead has been constituted by chairs of boards, the presidential triumvirate,[31] and other appointed (not elected) trustees, drawn from the sub-systems of the Society. This has ensured a model of governance at total odds with what today should be a well-structured and legally compliant charity. Those currently on the BoT should be *accountable* to trustees, who are independent of the Society. Instead, in the BPS at present, they *are* the trustees. Even for well-intentioned people of good faith, this inevitably leads to conflicts of interest and forms of rhetoric that defend them (the bullshit I describe in Chapter 7).

This problem of conflicts of interest and lack of independence returns, like a bad penny, and is discussed often in the chapters to come. Moreover, as well as this lack of proper independent oversight, a new political dynamic was emerging at the turn of this century. If the earlier years in the Society were characterised by tensions between applied and pure psychologists, now *managerialism* created the prospects of a controlling group[32] who were, by and large, not psychologists.

Members of the new senior management team (after 2018) were neither elected nor appointed to the Board, but employed by the Society, on high salaries. They came face to face with the old system (of non-independent trustees), triggering a new political scenario. Would the new managers be accountable to the Board, keeping it informed and seeking its ultimate approval for their actions? Alternatively, might a new prospect be that they were to keep trustees in the dark, when and if required? Might they simply ask or seek 'rubber-stamping', rather than expecting to be accountable to the Board of Trustees? Put simply, who was now 'in charge' of the BPS?

Remember that there were no independent trustees present to judge and moderate the implications of this incipient power struggle.

Managers could come and go, holding extensive temporary power but having no inkling of academic values in general or the complex character of psychology in particular. Whereas managers in any organisation are concerned with defending a preferred view of reality, this can soon err in the direction of censorship (I pick up this point in Chapter 7). Censorship is fundamentally at odds with academic values, but managers who move from one (non-academic) employer to another may well be ignorant of these norms and expectations. Managerialism tends to encourage propaganda, not truth seeking, when and if its own powers are under threat.

As will be clear throughout this book, sadly a picture of managerial best practice, expected of a well-run charity, has been absent from the leadership culture in the BPS. Some managers were not even familiar with working in the charity sector but came from private industry or local authorities. This scenario, of 'managers-for-hire' moving from one setting to another, would not auger well for dealing with the complex tensions bequeathed by the history of British psychology noted earlier. That combination of ignorance and arrogance from these managerial carpetbaggers was to become a toxic mix, to add to the problem of lack of trustee independence present since 1965.

The recent past

The starting summary offered at the beginning of the chapter, describing the current crisis, now has a context of emergence, which can be outlined as follows.

1. The BPS has contained the epistemological contradictions of being at the cusp of natural and social science.
2. The BPS has contained the political contradictions of representing professional psychologists (the Divisions), while also claiming, with diminishing credibility, to be a learned Society (the Sections and Boards). The organisation rides two horses, one professional and the other disciplinary. Sometimes they stray in different directions, with painful consequences for the rider.
3. The BPS has evolved over a period of more than a century, under the fluxing external influence of its host society. Two major wars and the

subsequent emergence of neoliberalism, managerialism, and latterly identity politics, in the wake of the postmodern turn, have all in their own way left their mark. We are left wondering what Ward and Rivers would make of the crisis today and the fate of their naïve, de-contextualised form of scientific realism.

4. The existence of a BoT, which since 1965 has failed to offer true independent oversight, has afforded misgovernance and corruption. This major strategic failure on the part of the Society's leaders at that time to ensure and embed genuine independent oversight created the conditions of possibility for the legitimation crisis of today.

After the missed opportunity for governance reform in 1988, two examples can be given of reaping what was sown in relation to the final point. First, the triumph of holding a register (Newman's bombastic celebration) was short-lived. In 2003, the Health and Care Professions Council (HCPC) was established, and the BPS then ceded its regulatory power to this new body.[33]

The complaints procedure designed to ensure that the good intentions of the Code of Conduct of the Society were put into practice, for all intents and purposes, now fell into disuse. The BPS website informed the public that complaints against individual members could *not* be investigated. And yet, in an example of gross hypocrisy and short-term self-interest, those running the Society opted to investigate a particular member who was legitimately challenging their power. They expelled the elected but critical president, Nigel MacLennan. For reasons of *sub judice*, a fuller discussion of his treatment is not offered here, though I return to the matter at the end of the book.

Second, if there is no independent oversight in any charity, then it is only a matter of time before financial inefficiency gives way to irregularity and then eventually full-blown corruption. Since the turn of this century, this has been one feature of the BPS, meaning that its leaders have arguably *already* brought their own organisation into disrepute, even if this fact has been shrouded from public scrutiny.

In an attempt to re-establish its authoritative role as a regulatory body, recently the BPS has made a bid to take charge of an emerging group of mental health workers. This move, given the crisis outlined above, is audacious but also makes sense for the current leadership if the bid works. It would bring into the fold *many new fee-paying* members, in line both with treating the Society as a money-making business and with the norms of an NPM culture. It might also serve as a diversionary tactic in relation to the legitimation crisis and gives the semblance of building a better future for the Society, by expanding its provenance. The organisational risk of a recently management-favoured 'stack-'em-high' approach to finance is addressed by Pat Harvey, in her commentary at the end of Chapter 8.

What is important to note about this move to income expansion is that that those in the targeted workforce do not have to be psychology graduates. This would undermine a central tradition of the minimum criterion of grounds for membership. The boundary between professionals and amateurs, installed when the BPS set itself apart from the laity in 1906, would now become porous.

Whether this marks social progress is a matter of opinion, raising a wider question about whether middle-class professionals are a boon or not to society.[34] However, what is clear is that non-psychologists might now be part of an organisation, with its remaining and faltering rhetorical claims to be a learned body. For good or bad, its members will now have a hotchpotch of credentials, leaving the public with little clarity of the significance of BPS membership in a named individual.

Conclusion

This opening chapter has set the scene for the rest of the book. The following chapters will spell out the recent implications of the historical and ideological forces that have shaped British psychology in the past hundred years. More importantly, they will justify why the notion of 'legitimation crisis' is not merely fanciful hyperbole. Currently, the BPS is in serious trouble because of historical forces that triggered its poor governance. To quote William Faulkner, 'The past is never dead. It's not even past.'[35] However, those in charge currently of the BPS are prone to ignore this insight, in favour of 'drawing a line under the past' and looking instead, Pollyanna fashion, to the future alone.[36] They are following in the British leadership tradition of Lord Nelson, when placing the telescope to his blind eye.[37]

The cliché that to ignore the problems of the past typically ensures their repetition is also a wise truism. Self-serving 'line drawing' is a common trope in modern managerialism, with its proneness to 'impression management' and 'bullshit', a topic I return to in Chapter 7. It undermines the development of *phronesis* (authentic wisdom) and ensures that the Society cannot become a learning organisation. In order to learn, we have to be honest about both current problems and their antecedent conditions of possibility, requiring trust-building for all concerned. As will be clear in the coming pages, those running the BPS in recent decades have signally failed in this regard.

The critics writing in this book continue to campaign for radical governance reform and honesty about failures to date. At the time of writing, it is not clear whether those efforts at critical feedback will be effective. Instead, the Society may be in terminal decline and prone to fragmentation; the formation of the ABP in 2000 and ACP in 2017 may have been a harbinger of this trend. We shall see in the coming months and years.

Notes

1. The challenge of achieving and sustaining legitimacy has been explored by both political sociologists and social psychologists: J. Habermas (1973). *Legitimation Crisis*; J. Jost & B. Major (Eds.) (2001). *The Psychology of Legitimacy: Emerging Perspectives on Ideology, Justice, and Intergroup Relations*. Cambridge: Cambridge University Press.

2. From its website: 'We register and regulate charities in England and Wales, to ensure that the public can support charities with confidence. Charity Commission is a non-ministerial department.'

3. The BPS today has an estimated membership of around 67,000, which at the time of writing the SMT want to augment substantially with non-psychology graduates.

4. Those in this group were not aware at first of Nigel MacLennan's marginalisation and scapegoating but after a few months made contact with him and then continued to provide him with support.

5. Hermeneutics is the science of interpretations.

6. The hegemony of the position of Ward and Rivers was repeated until the 1960s in standard psychology textbooks—see, for example, R. S. Woodworth & D. G. Marquis (1947). *Psychology: A Study of Mental Life*. London: Methuen.

7. Editorial from James Ward and William Rivers, *British Journal of Psychology* (1904), *1*(1): 1.
8. L. S. Hearnshaw (1964). *A Short History of British Psychology*. London: Methuen; 'Biographical Notes on the Ten Founding Members', published in H. Steinberg (Ed.) (1961). *The British Psychological Society 1901–1961*, Supplement to the *Bulletin of the British Psychological Society*.
9. These are described in P. L. Berger & T. Luckmann (1966). *The Social Construction of Reality: A Treatise on the Sociology of Knowledge*. Garden City, New York: Anchor Books.
10. By 1902, the Society had only thirteen members, and even by the outbreak of the First World War, there were only seventy-nine.
11. Hearnshaw, *A Short History of British Psychology*.
12. This challenge of British empiricism undermining theory-building and philosophical confidence in the academy prompted the needed importation of both ideas and intellectuals from abroad during the twentieth century. Examples in psychology were Hans Eysenck and Monte Shapiro, and in philosophy we found Ludwig Wittgenstein and Karl Popper; P. Anderson (1969). Components of the national culture. *New Left Review, 50* July/August. The central role of Eysenck is considered in Chapter 8.
13. For the past fifty years, a number of commentators have noted that psychology has been prone not to one but many forms of crisis, e.g., G. S. Howard (1986). *Dare We Develop a Human Science?* Notre Dame, IN: Academic Publications; B. Hughes (2016). *Psychology In Crisis*. London: Red Globe Press; and G. Westland (1978). *Current Crises in Psychology*. London: Heinemann.
14. Popper's critical rationalism rejected naïve empiricism; K. Popper (1962). *Conjectures and Refutations: The Growth of Scientific Knowledge*. New York: Basic Books. Post-Popperian revisions, in opposition to the postmodern turn, can be found as well now in critical realism; D. Pilgrim (2020). *Critical Realism for Psychologists*. London: Routledge.
15. Cited in L. P. Pojman & P. Tramel (2009). *Moral Philosophy: A Reader*. New York: Hackett.
16. H. J. Eysenck (1985). *Decline and Fall of the Freudian Empire*. London: Penguin.
17. D. Pilgrim (2008). The eugenic legacy in psychology and psychiatry. *International Journal of Social Psychiatry, 54*(3), 272–284. This point is picked up again in Chapter 10.

18. For example, do people work harder at a task the more you pay them? The amount of payment is the independent variable and their performance on the task is the dependent variable.

19. Compare the roots of modern positivism and its notion of fixity, and purported lawful relationships across time and space, with the idea of fluxing open systems. All human systems are open not closed. The fixity position was offered by one pre-Socratic thinker, Parmenides, and challenged by another, Heraclitus, who suggested that: 'A man cannot step into the same river twice, for fresh waters ever emerge around him.' Note that both the man changes and so does the river. Today, any psychologist, pure or applied, might reflect on which ancient thinker was wiser, Parmenides or Heraclitus.

20. For an overview, see J. Cromby & D. J. Nightingale (1999). What's wrong with social constructionism? In D. J. Nightingale and J. Cromby (Eds.), *Social Constructionist Psychology: A Critical Analysis of Theory and Practice*. Buckingham: Open University Press.

21. Z. Gao (2014). Methodologism/methodological imperative. In T. Teo (Ed.), *Encyclopaedia of Critical Psychology* (pp. 1189–1193). New York, NY: Springer.

22. British sociology too has struggled to reconcile the tendencies of realism and constructivism and their competing affordances of quantitative and qualitative methods. Methodologism in that discipline has been less evident though than the tendency to retreat into social theory as a perceived prestigious alternative to empirical investigations of *any* sort.

23. D. Pilgrim & A. Treacher (1992). *Clinical Psychology Observed*. London: Routledge.

24. J. Hall, D. Pilgrim, & G. Turpin (Eds.) (2015). *Clinical Psychology in Britain: Historical Perspectives*. HoPC Monograph No. 2. Leicester: British Psychological Society.

25. Renamed the 'Association of Business Psychology' in 2013.

26. D. Smith (2014). *Under New Public Management: Institutional Ethnographies of Changing Front-Line Work*. Toronto: University of Toronto Press.

27. The BPS Council oversaw the BoT. In recent years, it has been replaced by a smaller 'Senate'.

28. C. Newman (1988). *Evolution and Revolution*, charter guide, occasional paper. Leicester: British Psychological Society.

29. www.bps.org.uk/sites/bps.org.uk/files/How%20we%20work/BPS %20Royal%20Charter%20and%20Statues.

30. Independence means a trustee being in a position to walk away from the role, with no financial or career status implications for them.

31. The president is elected by the BPS membership. For one year, they are the president elect, then they are president for a year and then vice president for another. Thus, at a point in time, the BoT contains three different elected people with those separate titles.

32. In the BPSWatch blog, we have alluded often to a 'cabal' today, predicated on an 'oligarchy' from the past.

33. Only a minority of BPS members are eligible to be on the HCPC register. Credential criteria for being a neuropsychologist or a health psychologist are set by the BPS and may be required for employment purposes, but there is no disciplinary infrastructure in place to receive complaints. Given that the BPS claims to retain a credible Code of Practice, but at the same time it disavows the power to investigate complaints against individual members, currently there is a large regulatory (and credibility) gap. For example, when a complaint is made about an academic psychologist, the complainant is typically referred back to the employer of the accused for investigation. Thus, those members who are not *applied* psychologists are regulated weakly or even not at all by the BPS.

34. Durkheim depicted the professions as being a progressive source of social integration and moral regulation. Weber and Marx were more ambivalent, especially the former. (See G. Carchedi (1975). On the economic identification of the new middle class. *Economy and Society, 4*(1), 1–85; M. Saks (1983). Removing the blinkers? A critique of recent contributions to the sociology of the professions. *The Sociological Review, 31*(1), 1–21.)

35. W. Faulkner (1951). *Requiem for a Nun.* New York: Random House.

36. See the resurgence of this Pollyanna approach denying the current crisis and its historical roots in a joint statement from the president installed to replace Nigel MacLennan, Katherine Carpenter, and the CEO returning from suspension: *The Psychologist,* January 2022, 4–5. The only safe concession to considering history is the safe marketing strategy to reject Galtonian eugenics (the Spearman Medal and the Annual Eysenck Memorial Lecture have now been abandoned). I return to this matter in Chapter 8.

37. Though Churchill, another British leader, offered his version of the adage from George Santayana, 'Those who do not remember the past are condemned to repeat it.'

CHAPTER 2

The lure of the toxic leader

Graham Buchanan

In 2013, Reverend Paul Flowers, chairman of the Co-operative Bank, hit the headlines when he was caught out seeking to purchase cocaine and methamphetamine. Amongst other, more lurid, revelations, the bank lost £700m in the first half of 2013, and Flowers resigned in May 2013. A further £1.5 billion hole in the bank's finances was discovered by the new chief executive in May 2013. A Labour MP, who knew the flamboyant sixty-three-year-old, said, 'He loved the limelight and I suppose, well, people just thought: that's Paul.'[1]

On Saturday, 23 November 2013, Daniel Boffey and Jill Treanor wrote in *The Guardian*: 'That slight unease, sometimes made audible at Co-op meetings in the form of a nervous laugh at the chairman's latest extravagance, or a gentle tut-tut at his florid language and over-bearing nature, has metamorphosed into a veritable roar of outrage in the past week.'[2] This was of particular interest to me because I was secretary of the British Academy of Management Special Interest Group on Corporate Governance with a personal focus on corporate ethics.

We all know the ancient adage, 'With great power comes great responsibility', but some leaders seem to confuse power with entitlement and that is a toxic combination.

Toxic leadership

For many years, leadership programmes have focused on what makes a 'great leader' by exploring the uniqueness of any number of great leaders. In fact, what we have been attempting to achieve is actually unachievable because you can't mimic those special things that make great leaders unique. Instead, my focus fell on what constitutes 'bad' leadership, particularly toxicity. But what is the difference between simply bad leadership and toxic leadership? The simple answer is outcomes. A bad leader can still produce good outcomes; a toxic leader causes lasting damage to the organisation, and the people in it, financially, reputationally, legally, and emotionally.

Some years ago, I was holding a plenary session when a senior leader asked: 'Why do we spend so much time talking about "vision" when it is such a waste of time?'

Because effective leaders always have a vision, but perhaps not the sort of vision that he was alluding to. Effective leaders have 'noble visions' that demonstrate fine personal qualities and high moral principles. Their route to the end game is often long and tortuous (for example, Nelson Mandela), but a 'toxic leader' doesn't have any such thing. They merely have a 'grand illusion' that seeks to achieve quick, ultimately valueless wins which people willingly buy into. The illusion taps into public concerns and/or personal greed, until such time as the penny drops, by which time it's often too late. Ultimately, the motivation of the 'toxic leader' is entirely selfish. They say and do little or nothing for the common good. In short, a toxic leader costs in every sense of the word.

This is how I define a toxic leader: as a person who has responsibility for a group, organisation, or situation, who abuses the leader–stakeholder relationship by leaving the stakeholders in a worse condition than they were prior to the leader's intervention.

This is not about momentary bad management, negligence, or incompetence. It is a continuous course of conduct which, if it isn't interrupted or diverted, will be destructive to all stakeholders as they seek to subvert and destroy structures in pursuit of their 'grand illusion'.

People often ask why toxic leaders aren't rumbled early in their careers. The simple answer is that toxic leaders are masters at building support in the early stages of their career to the point where they are virtually fireproof, when they can unleash their toxicity on the weak and unsuspecting.

In 1867, philosopher John Stuart Mill delivered the inaugural address at the University of St Andrews and stated: 'Bad men need nothing more to compass their ends, than that good men should look on and do nothing.'[3]

While true in essence, this is too simplistic because you can only oppose what you can clearly see, and toxic leaders keep their intentions hidden by obfuscation, deceit, and smoke and mirrors. Moreover, no one person has a grasp of the complete picture, and members of the organisation aren't talking to each other because they don't want to be seen as disloyal. Anyway, in a truly toxic environment, who do you actually trust?

A 'toxic organisation' is one that has a 'toxic leader' and numerous 'toxic followers' who willingly carry out the toxic leader's wishes without complaint or objection, and that is the nub of the problem. Toxic leaders only succeed because other people don't just stand by and do nothing, *they* actively support the toxic leader in their venture. Below, I consider the importance of complicit 'followship' that must support toxic leaders for a toxic organisational culture to grow.

The toxic leader's intention

Toxic leaders spend a lifetime acquiring power to ensure their own particular grand illusion is implemented and, once they have sufficient power, they will use whatever means necessary to cling onto to it. Loyalty for a toxic leader means nothing—they don't care who they crush to keep hold of power, even their own supposed followers.

And there is a reason for this attitude.

The dark triad

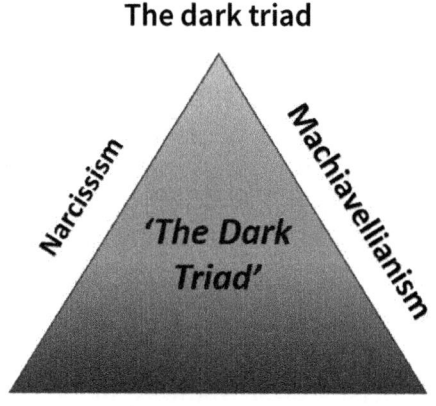

Psychopathy

All leaders are narcissistic to a degree. They like the plaudits, the acclaim, and the fame. What they don't all do is engage in Machiavellian activities to either retain the thrill or acquire more of it. They have a little more empathy than that—see diagram above.

In her 1990 essay 'Freedom from Fear', Aung San Suu Kyi wrote: 'It is not power that corrupts, but fear. Fear of losing power corrupts those who wield it and fear of the scourge of power corrupts those who are subject to it.'

But, in light of recent events in Myanmar, who really held the power while she was president? Was it really her, or was it General Min Aung Hlaing, commander-in-chief of the armed forces, who lost to Aung San Suu Kyi in the 2011 presidential election? It would appear he always had the power, as she has now been sentenced to two years' imprisonment.

The list of leaders who have abused the leader–stakeholder relationship in world history is extensive, but is it merely rampant ambition or is it something else? We can all explore this question from our own experience. As an icebreaker at the Leadership Academy, I would pose a question to the group on the very first day of the first module, and the question was: In two or three words, how do you see yourself as a leader?

I would usually get a mix of answers such as 'transformational', 'strategic', 'positive', 'dynamic', 'charismatic', and so on. In fact, all the labels they probably thought I would like to hear, but one surprised me because he wrote: 'Not pink and fluffy!'

I posed another question to the group: 'If I were to ask your staff the same question, what answer do you think they would give?'

He again wrote: 'Not pink and fluffy!'

A specific question to him: 'In any circumstance?'

His answer: 'None!'

His colleagues looked as surprised as I was and, over the course of the week, he demonstrated zero empathy and zero emotional intelligence, prompting my colleague to comment: 'You wouldn't want to work for a man like that!'

Which prompted me to respond: 'And you wouldn't want to cross a man like that!'

And this is often the reason why people do not speak out: they are afraid. Toxic leaders spend years acquiring power, and they spend years learning what strategies are best to implement their power. In short, their moral compass is skewed.

Morals, ethics, values, and 'toxicity'

In this context, 'morals' are society's norms—they define what's 'right' or 'wrong', 'legal' or 'illegal'; 'ethics' are the higher standards we expect of people in 'positions of power', that is, in leadership positions—but it's not as clear cut as being merely 'right' or 'wrong', hence we have 'ethical dilemmas'.

'Values' are the belief systems that shape an individual's actions, whether for good or bad, some of which are their predominant core values—the values that are so vital to their wellbeing that they may struggle to overcome them. I do not doubt that Paul Flowers knew that what he was doing was wrong, but he couldn't overcome his predominant core values (see Chapter 8 for the distinction between the liar and the bullshitter).

How extensive is toxicity?

'Toxicity' applies where a person (or even an organisation) is emotionally disengaged from both the moral and ethical norms of society and whose predominant core values are, ultimately, highly damaging. When it spreads as an organisational culture, this will lead to recurring outcomes.

A look at employment tribunal statistics shows that claims are soaring across the board. This might be because people are far more willing to make a claim or because organisational behaviour has deteriorated markedly. The bland data don't indicate one way or another, but do demonstrate a worrying trend. For example, three of the top four reasons are discrimination (up 220 per cent), whistleblowing (up 141 per cent), and unfair dismissal (up 119 per cent).[4]

Some commentators have attempted to explain the rise of employment tribunal cases on 'toxic leadership', and while there may be an element of truth in that, most suggestions don't bear close scrutiny. 'Toxicity' is far too complicated for such bland descriptions.

Furthermore, it is far too simplistic to look at the extremes of toxic leadership such as Hitler, Stalin, Pol Pot, and so on, and say "I don't behave like them so I am not toxic"; but most toxic leaders are not like them. Most toxic leaders are unethical, lacking both empathy and emotional intelligence, but they are not 'evil' in the purest sense of the word.

But every leader has a little bit of 'toxicity' in them. We have all done things that, with the benefit of hindsight, we wouldn't have done. We have all been a bit incompetent, or parochial, or snappy with people, but this is not 'toxic leadership'. We are just not performing up to scratch, and there are any number of reasons why people can become temporarily 'toxic'.

True toxic leadership is a *continuing course of action* that adversely impacts on both stakeholders and the organisation that is repeated time and again, with little or no concern for its harmful consequences. It is important to understand that toxic leadership occurs everywhere—in public, private, and voluntary organisations.

For example, take the GPO sub-postmaster scandal. On 26 April 2021, Coreena Ford reported on BusinessLive:

> Hundreds of sub-postmasters were prosecuted for theft, fraud and false accounting because of the Post Office's defective Horizon accounting system, which had 'bugs, defects and errors' from the very outset.
>
> On Friday, 39 former sub-postmasters who were convicted and even jailed based on Horizon data had their convictions overturned by the Court of Appeal.[5]

In December 2019, the Post Office paid out £58 million to compensate some sub-postmasters. The judge presiding on the case, Mr Justice Fraser, described the Post Office's approach to the case as 'institutional obstinacy' that:

amounted, in reality, to bare assertions and denials that ignore what has actually occurred, at least so far as the witnesses called before me in the Horizon Issues trial are concerned. It amounts to the 21st century equivalent of maintaining that the earth is flat.[6]

In January 2020, Paula Vennells's tenure as Post Office CEO was strongly criticised by Conservative peer Lord Arbuthnot:

> The hallmark of Paula Vennells' time as CEO was that she was willing to accept appalling advice from people in her management and legal teams. The consequences of this were far-reaching for the Post Office and devastating for the sub-postmasters. However, there seem to have been no consequences for her.[7]

He described the behaviour of the Post Office under her leadership as 'both cruel and incompetent', and said that 'she was faced with a moral choice and she took the wrong one, the one which allowed hundreds of sub-postmasters to be falsely accused, humiliated and ruined by the organisation she ran'.[8]

On 26 November 2021, *The Daily Telegraph* reported: 'Post Office value slashed to zero after postmasters' scandal—£233m compensation payouts over Horizon scandal leave institution worthless.'

Leaders, ethics, and toxic followship

Except for those who have a genuine interest in the subject, few leaders really get the point of ethics. It is rarely discussed at board or senior management level. At best, it may be discussed occasionally, but little credence is attached to it.

Senior leaders may get the point of 'toxicity' from their experience, and they may even have learnt from it. However, a toxic leader very rarely sees it in themselves, particularly if they are perceived as 'successful'. When they are confronted with the blindingly obvious, they delay, defer, obfuscate, deny, redact, until such time as there is nowhere else left to hide.

Furthermore, toxic leaders cannot thrive, or sustain momentum, without people who are prepared to support them in their toxicity, a point I return to below.

The history of 'toxic leaders'

The term was first used in 1972 when the American Academy of Psychotherapists' journal *Voice* (8: 32–33) recorded:

> The toxic leader rejects or neglects the importance of his role as a major determinant of how the group will function ... The toxic leader 'accepts' whatever happens in or to the group. Other toxic leaders endeavor to manipulate the group to enhance their own egos.

In her 1996 book *Toxic Leaders: When Organisations Go Bad*, Professor Marcia Lynn Whicker defined a toxic leader as: 'someone who has responsibility over a group of people or an organisation, and who abuses the leader-follower relationship leaving the group, or organisation, in a worse off condition than when they found them'.

She described good leadership as 'pervasive, persuasive and persistent', and bad leadership as 'poisoned with pedanticism, posturing, self-importance'.

The seven bad behaviours

In *Bad Leadership: What It Is, How It Happens, Why It Matters* (2004), Professor Barbara Kellerman suggests that 'bad leadership' may be analysed into seven different types:

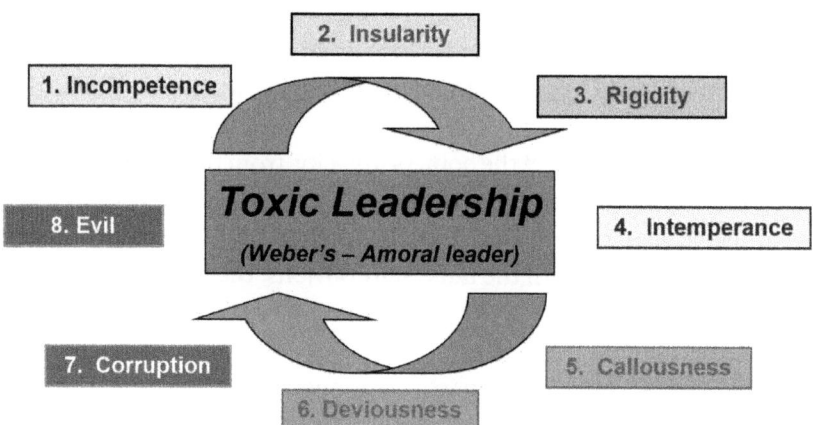

But at what point does 'bad leadership' become toxic? Simply put, all of it is 'toxic' if it leads to defined outcomes. The notion that there is 'less bad' is erroneous.

'Incompetent' can easily turn to something more serious if the incompetence causes serious pain and damage to others. It is exacerbated when, knowing that is the case, the toxic leader then obfuscates, denies, defers, etc., in an attempt to absolve themselves of any responsibility for the outcome.

It would appear that former Post Office CEO Paula Vennells sits in at least four of Kellerman's 'bad leadership' types. A toxic leader can be any, or all, of the above, and the more toxic the leader, the more of these characteristics they are likely to display, but a leader who incorporates all seven is a very rare breed indeed, and is often someone who has 'morally disengaged', not just from the people they are leading, but from society at large.

Interestingly, studies have shown that, although we can readily identify toxic leaders, we tend to do very little about them until the situation becomes intolerable at a personal level. In other words, we soak up the grief until we can stand it no longer.

In *The Allure of Toxic Leaders: Why We Follow Destructive Bosses and Corrupt Politicians—and How We Can Survive Them* (2006), Professor Lipman-Blumen explains that there was, and still is, a tendency among contemporary society to seek authoritative, even dominating, characteristics among our corporate and political leaders because of the public's own personal psychosocial needs and emotional weaknesses.

She reinforces the point that 'toxic leadership' is not about run-of-the-mill mismanagement—rather, it refers to leaders who, by virtue of their 'dysfunctional personal characteristics' and 'destructive behaviours … inflict reasonably serious and enduring harm', not only on their own followers and organisations, but on others outside of their immediate circle of victims and subordinates.

Professor Terry L. Price takes a slightly different view. In *Understanding Ethical Failures in Leadership* (2005), he says: 'Leaders can know that a behaviour is … required by morality, but be mistaken as to whether it applies to them … and whether others are protected by it.'

Fred Goodwin, Gordon Brown, James Murdoch, Sharon Shoesmith, Lord Blair, and Martin Yeates all provoked moral outrage for one reason or another, but who is truly toxic, and who simply had a bad day at the office?

Conversely, Jimmy Savile is on a truly different scale of evilness, but he got away with it for so long because people were afraid to confront him, despite the fact that numerous allegations had been made against him. He spent years acquiring toxic power and developed highly effective strategies to use it. He built a smokescreen of caring, volunteering, philanthropy, 'fixing it', to exercise his toxic power over at least 450 victims. It was only a year after his death that the full scale of his offending came to light.

Kate Lampard and Ed Marsden's 2015 report into lessons to be learned from the health service's handling of the Savile scandal concluded that:

> Savile was a highly unusual personality whose lifestyle, behaviour and offending patterns were equally unusual. As a result of his celebrity, his volunteering, and his fundraising he had exceptional access to a number of NHS hospitals and took the opportunities that that access gave him to abuse patients, staff and others on a remarkable scale. Savile's celebrity and his roles as a volunteer and fundraiser also gave him power and influence within NHS hospitals which meant that his behaviour, which was often evidently inappropriate, was not challenged as it should have been.[9]

'Values shape leaders; leaders shape cultures'

A toxic leader creates a toxic culture which is driven by their predominant core values. If left unchecked, a toxic leader will eventually generate a crisis of leadership, particularly if concerned followers fail to act early enough.

Because, if left unchecked, toxicity grows until it becomes embedded in the very fabric of the organisation and is totally unmanageable without major structural reform (e.g., Yorkshire Cricket Club, where sixteen members of staff, including the entire coaching team, left following racism allegations made by former player Azeem Rafiq after a period of success for the team).

Michael O'Byrne, the former chief constable of Bedfordshire Police, said: 'When performance walks through one door, ethics often walks out of another.'

And toxicity invariably walks in a third if targets, profits, and the bottom line are the only measures of performance.

Fred Goodwin certainly left the RBS in a 'worse off condition than when he found it', but that was okay for a while because he created the illusion of massive growth and wealth and the accolades poured in.

In December 2002, he was Forbes (global edition) 'Businessman of the Year', described as an 'original thinker with a fast-forward frame of mind who had transformed RBS from a nonentity into a global name'. From 2003 to 2006, he was No. 1 in *Scotland on Sunday*'s Power 100. In December 2003, he became 'European Banker of the Year'. In 2004, he was knighted in the Queen's Birthday Honours List. In June 2004, he was awarded an honorary Doctor of Law by the University of St Andrews. In 2005, he was criticised by some RBS shareholders for putting global expansion ahead of short-term financial returns. In July 2008, he was awarded an honorary fellowship by the London Business School. And yet RBS lost £24 billion on his watch and was effectively nationalised to stop it going under.

What follower would, or could, have confronted a man as 'successful' as Goodwin? Who would have possibly believed what they were saying?

How toxic leadership operates

Toxic leadership creates a toxic culture where 'toxicity' becomes endemic and followers either feel powerless to stop it or actively join in to advance their own agenda. This creates the conditions of possibility for a culture of 'bullshit', explored in Chapter 8.

To function, a toxic leader must create a fertile environment where toxicity can thrive, and this occurs where there is low resistance from fellow leaders and stakeholders which, ultimately, reinforces the fertile toxic environment. We can look for the following key indicators of a 'fertile toxic environment':

1. Vague, or absent, mission, vision, and, particularly, values to guide the organisation.
2. Limited mutual respect and social bonding; staff co-exist rather than cooperate.

3. Staff are micro-managed rather than trusted; there is no legitimate *esprit de corps* whereby everybody pulls together (as per Henri Fayol); silo mentalities predominate.
4. There are inconsistent rewards; an 'I'm all right, Jack' mentality; a culture of 'performance is everything', but what 'performance' looks like isn't clearly defined.
5. 'Timid' senior executives/board members who won't challenge; there is no personal 'integrity' or responsibility—sycophants abound.
6. No clear cultural boundaries which define the organisation; there is no sense of what is right and wrong because there is no 'line in the sand'.
7. There is no sense of vocation and, hence, no emotional investment in the organisation, resulting in high levels of absenteeism and 'churn'.

Greg Dyke, the former director general of the BBC, said: 'Leadership is about the stories that are told about you—both positive and negative.'[10] For example, Boris Johnson had a relatively good COP26. He successfully faced down President Macron over fishing rights, and then blew it with the fiasco over his attempt to 'rescue' Owen Patterson from Kathryn Stone OBE, the parliamentary commissioner for standards.

The 5 November 2021 edition of *The Sun* described his actions as a 'Flip flopalypse'. This followed on from the Dominic Cummings/ Barnard Castle saga; opposing Marcus Rashford's demand for free school meals during lockdown; and Matt Hancock's notorious clinch with his aide Gina Coladangelo, but the Owen Patterson faux pas was a step too far for Tory MPs. *The Sun* went on to say:

> [Tory MPs'] targets were for Chief Whip Mark Spencer and Mr. Rees Mogg with MPs accusing them of egging the PM on with his 'stupid' plan.
>
> One senior Tory said: 'It has been a total s***show. He looks like an idiot, and we all look like idiots. How dumb do you have to be?
>
> 'The problem with Boris is that he packs his cabinet with second-rate people, meaning there is no one to tell him he should take a different course.'[11]

Then, to cap it all, he took a private jet back from COP26 to go to a private reunion dinner for *Daily Telegraph* journalists at the men-only

Garrick Club, after warning world leaders 'it's one minute to midnight to prevent climate catastrophe'.

Remember, your leadership is ultimately defined by the stories people tell about you, because it's very difficult to come back from being perceived as, at best, lacking judgement or competence or, worse, being accused of sleaze and cronyism. So Boris became the story, rather than the government's policies.

Dr Karen Y. Wilson-Starks, the president and CEO of Transleadership Inc., said in 2003: 'toxic leaders disseminate their poison through over-control. They define leadership as being "in control".'[12]

Does 'toxicity' rely on the leader being in total control—the micromanager who has to have an input in everything, even on the most mundane topics? Not so. Boris is perceived as incompetent, and he has made a career of being a carefully crafted 'buffoon', but his MPs now view his buffoonery as 'toxic'. So do some leaders have certain characteristics that lend themselves to toxicity?

The dark triad

In their 2002 article, 'The dark triad of personality: Narcissism, Machiavellianism, and psychopathy' in *The Journal of Research in Personality*, Paulhus and Williams pointed out that 'the dark triad of personality' comprises the malevolent personality traits of narcissism, Machiavellianism, and psychopathy, and that people scoring high on these traits are more likely to commit crimes, cause social distress, and, particularly from our perspective, create severe problems for an organisation, especially if they are in leadership positions.

They also tend to be less compassionate, agreeable, empathetic, satisfied with their lives, and less likely to believe they and others are good.

All three 'dark triad' traits are conceptually distinct, although empirical evidence shows them to be overlapping. They are associated with a callous-manipulative interpersonal style.

- Narcissism is characterised by grandiosity, pride, egotism, and a lack of empathy. It is self-centred, having an excessive interest in one's physical appearance and an excessive preoccupation with one's own needs, often at the expense of others.

- Machiavellianism is characterised by manipulation and exploitation of others, an absence of morality, unemotional callousness, and a higher level of self-interest. It is a personality trait that denotes cunning and a drive to use whatever means necessary to gain power.
- Psychopathy is characterised by persistent antisocial behaviour, impulsivity, selfishness, callous and unemotional traits, and remorselessness. It is defined as an antisocial disorder in which an individual manifests amoral and antisocial behaviour, shows a lack of ability to love or establish meaningful personal relationships, expresses extreme egocentricity, and demonstrates a failure to learn from experience.

All three traits share characteristics such as a lack of empathy, interpersonal hostility, and interpersonal offensiveness.

So, are all leaders an embodiment of the 'dark triad'? Although those with these features can be found as lawyers, surgeons, police officers, clergy, and civil servants, not all in their ranks are amoral schemers. Most have learned to control their psychopathic tendencies (which, to a degree, we all have). Furthermore, we all have a little narcissism in us, but that doesn't mean we are toxic. It is often the driver for us to achieve more. What we must have as good leaders is emotional intelligence, which is precluded by the 'dark triad'.

Emotional intelligence, and by definition empathy, is concerned with achieving self and social mastery by being smart with your core emotions. Self-mastery is a combination of being aware of your core emotions and then learning to manage them. It is a matter of developing empathy for others and having the social skills to act upon it. Toxic leaders are deficient in both, but this means they are also deficient elsewhere.

Noble visions or grand illusions

Great leaders have 'noble visions' that people understand and buy into; toxic leaders have 'grand illusions' which are sold at a price. But great leaders aren't gods. They err too, but they tend to win big and lose small and are ultimately defined by their legacy, and that must have a basis in ethical leadership. Nor do great leaders have to appeal to everybody, but they have to appeal to a sufficient number to make a difference.

Toxic leaders, on the other hand, deploy extensive propaganda to achieve their aims. They use biased or misleading information to promote their own distorted agenda, and they can take a 'noble vision' and subvert it by an ignoble application.

Every leader is required to 'kiss the frog' occasionally; that is, to do something they really do not want to do, and that may mean dispensing with the services of unnecessary people and processes. Not nice, but sometimes necessary. Often, this is a judgement call based on the available evidence.

In fact, failing to 'kiss the frog' when necessary is consistent with Barbara Kellerman's definition of incompetence. Toxic leaders, on the other hand, are defined by the price *you* have to pay, not just economically, but emotionally and physically. They suck you dry.

Furthermore, toxic leaders 'breed' 'toxic followers' who then develop into toxic leaders in their own right. Like toxic leaders, toxic followers thrive on toxic messages, ignoring any that conflict with their own worldview. Surprisingly, toxic followers often despise their toxic leaders. They see them as competition and a threat, but the toxic leader provides them with what they need to both survive and thrive until they too can become toxic leaders.

In truth, toxic followers are quite willing and capable of sacrificing the toxic leader to get what they want but, then again, so are toxic leaders, and this battle creates an aura of fear due to the inherent insecurity of the organisation.

As a colleague said to me after visiting a particularly toxic environment: 'Sniff the air. It smells of fear!'

Options available to followers

Followers have four options:

1. 'Fight' the toxic system,
2. 'Flight': leave it entirely,
3. 'Freeze': keep their head down and go with the flow, or
4. 'Fawn': become a sycophant for an easy life.

But how many people who have worked for a toxic leader have actually complained, challenged, or blown the whistle on them? Very few,

I would suggest. Usually, they just leave and go somewhere else, allowing the toxic leader to continue unchallenged.

A toxic leader (and their followers) can have a significant and negative impact on an organisation, either directly or indirectly, and it will suffer as a result. The organisation may experience any or all of the following symptoms:

1. The organisation becomes 'politicised' in its broadest sense, leading to a high turnover of staff and high sickness rates.
2. The working environment is engendered by a general feeling of being 'unsafe'. This can manifest itself in many ways, but bullying behaviour is often widespread.
3. This results in low creativity and innovation, and little or no critical thinking and/or questioning.
4. There are excessive numbers of 'yes men' who won't challenge, even when they identify failures, because no one is prepared to put their head above the parapet.
5. There is excessive micromanagement with little focus on the 'bigger picture'.
6. Low staff morale proliferates, particularly feeling undervalued because staff don't get the rewards they feel they deserve for the effort they put in.
7. This all results in systemic damage to the organisation and failure to achieve the task.

The more of these consequences that show themselves, the more urgent the need for the organisation to act. There may have to be quite draconian action in order for the organisation to get back on an even keel.

'Fiduciary responsibilities' and 'toxic leaders'

An effective leader is a person who demonstrates a high degree of leadership skills commensurate with their role. Remember, the term 'leader' is very broad—it is 'a person in control of a group, an organisation, a country, or a specific situation'—so it can be anybody from the CEO to a supervisor or a member of the public taking charge at an incident.

'Bad' people can become 'bad' leaders (Kellerman, 2004), but they cannot demonstrate the basic leadership skills and qualities necessary to become truly effective. Primarily, they do not exercise their fiduciary responsibilities.

In a fiduciary relationship, a person who is in a position of vulnerability (i.e., a stakeholder), justifiably invests confidence, good faith, reliance, and trust in another person whose aid, advice, or protection is sought in some matter (i.e., a leader—the fiduciary).

In such a relationship, good conscience requires the fiduciary to act at all times for the sole benefit and interest of the one who trusts. It is a duty of care. A fiduciary duty is the highest standard of care in equity (of being fair and impartial) or of law. They are expected to be extremely loyal to the person to whom they owe the duty (the 'principal'), such that there must be no conflict of duty between the fiduciary and the principal.

Furthermore, the fiduciary must not profit from their position as a fiduciary, unless the principal (the stakeholders) consents, but this must be 'true consent'. That is, they mustn't take more than their salary, bonuses, and allowances in accordance with their contract (e.g., shareholders have a right to vote on executive remuneration).

'True consent' is consent that is readily given on the basis of known facts at the time it is given, but it is not true consent if the leader has provided false information, or worse, deliberately lied.

Moreover, there is a distinction between true consent and mere submission, acquiescence, or compliance, while under duress or pressure, or by fraud as to the nature of the circumstances provoking the consent.

An alternative way of looking at fiduciary responsibilities

Any person who is in a position of power over other people has a duty of care to use that power appropriately, responsibly, considerately, and proportionately. Some professions have a higher degree of fiduciary responsibility attached to them because of the higher degree of power they have over the people they interact with. As a consequence, there is a higher level of trust; hence the greater the moral outrage when they breach that trust. For example:

- Psychiatrist Dr Isaac 'Ike' Herschkopf who 'conned' a client out of $4.2 million;
- Dr Ian Patterson, jailed for twenty years for conducting unnecessary surgical procedures on more than 1,000 patients;

- Peter Ball, the Bishop of Gloucester, who abused eighteen young men;
- Wayne Couzens, who murdered Sarah Everard by abusing his position as a police officer; and
- Dr Harold Shipman, who may have killed up to 250 patients.

While these people had a fiduciary responsibility for the people in their care, they failed them because their own *wants* overtook the *needs* of their victims, and they deliberately exercised their power to satisfy those wants.

But it is not just individuals; organisations can have collective failures. The NHS has been the subject of scrutiny in relation to maternity care and, recently, the activities of the murderer and necrophiliac David Fuller, but it does not stand alone. The investigation into Wayne Couzens is ongoing.

In a 'toxic power' relationship, it isn't the 'crime' that is necessarily the issue (after all, many foul crimes are committed), it is the fact that the person has a position of fiduciary responsibility that causes the moral outrage, and this sense of moral outrage should be no less the case for toxic leaders.

Changing the toxic leader's approach?

When he visited the USA in 1959, Nikita Khrushchev was asked by a journalist why he had done nothing to prevent Stalin's atrocities. Khrushchev asked angrily, 'Who said that?' Nobody replied. He demanded again, 'Who said that?' Again, nobody replied. Khrushchev calmly said, 'That is precisely what I was doing.'

Changing a toxic leader's behaviours is a challenging, nigh on impossible proposition, particularly if they sit at the top of the tree (e.g., a Robert Maxwell, Conrad Black, or Fred Goodwin). Khrushchev wasn't prepared, or didn't have the moral courage, to speak out because he knew what the consequences would be for him. There is little difference between Khrushchev's approach and people who work in a toxic organisation and depend on it for their livelihood.

But, even if they were challenged, toxic leaders find it very difficult to reform because:

- They see no need to reform—they are, after all, successful, so why change?
- They see any suggestion of personal reform as an attack on their predominant core beliefs, so they do not see personal reform as having any value.
- Reform for a toxic leader usually requires a personal crisis, an epiphany event, that makes them see the world in a different way.
- But because 'epiphany events' are very rare, resistance to personal reform is inevitable.

Dealing with a toxic leader is even more difficult if they are performing a critical function on which the organisation depends and is not easy to replace, such as a recognised technical expert in their field. This, in itself, can provoke an ethical dilemma. Can the organisation survive and thrive without this individual? Conversely, can it continue to support someone who is toxic?

The only way to change them is to provoke a 'personal crisis', but acting for their benefit is also problematic. What could be done to provoke a 'personal crisis' that would be appropriate? Would a 'friendly chat' or removal of their bonus change them? Probably not, because they see no need to change.

One senior leader said to me that they would rather pay a toxic leader off than sustain continued damage to the organisation. Once the toxic leader was gone, toxic followers were much easier to deal with; the ambience of the organisation changed rapidly, and production, innovation, and morale improved considerably.

An example might be Sharon Shoesmith, formerly the Director of Children's Services in Hackney at the time of Baby P's death, but not for the reasons you may think. She was a very highly regarded leader who had held a number of senior positions and, as one very senior social worker informed me, she was 'tucked up like a kipper'.

Following the death of Baby P, Shoesmith didn't speak to the media for about a week, engaged a PR consultant, and then failed to exhibit an 'acceptable' level of contrition for her organisation's involvement in the death. In short, she wasn't good in front of a camera. She appeared evasive and defensive.

The public outcry was massive, and there was a real ethical dilemma on the part of the authorities. Do we sack her or don't we? In view of the public's moral outrage, it was felt that the only realistic course of action was to sack her, and without the pay-offs that someone in her position would usually expect to receive.

She took Hackney Council and Ed Balls, the minister who effectively sacked her, to court for wrongful dismissal and sex discrimination. She won her case and was awarded in excess of £600,000 (creating more moral outrage). This wasn't a case of whether Sharon Shoesmith was right or wrong in the circumstances, but whether the authorities were right in taking the action that they did. The public thought they were right, but the law didn't, so who was really 'toxic' in this situation?

Organisations may not care if an aggrieved individual takes them to court, and nor should they, but they must follow the correct procedures. The organisation will have rid themselves of a toxic leader, but just because they have walked out of the door does not mean the problem has gone away. Remember, their toxic followers are still there, and they will be vying for position.

So who is responsible for tackling toxicity?

The short answer is that we all are, but we have to live in an environment where we are able to do that. Too many organisations are too keen to protect their reputations to be open and honest about their problems. In reality, it is far better to be upfront, and take a short-term hit for a long-term gain. It is better to do something imperfectly than to do nothing perfectly.

My experience is that, in a culturally impoverished environment, you have to be proactive by attacking the causes and then building a 'culturally rich' environment where toxicity cannot thrive. You have to generate:

1. A clear intention, purpose, and core values that everybody understands.
2. Mutual respect and social bonding in any number of ways to help staff to know each other and to cooperate.
3. Trust in staff and *esprit de corps*. Break down silo mentalities and 'empires' that are expensive and produce little.

4. Rewards that are consistently applied against clearly defined targets for *that* area of responsibility.
5. Rewards that reflect 'doing the right thing', that is, innovation and questioning.
6. Positive leadership at all levels that is integrity-driven. Have no fear.
7. Clear cultural boundaries that define the organisation and clearly identify what is right and wrong—draw an organisational 'line in the sand'.
8. A sense of vocation; encourage emotional investment in the organisation—a sense of 'we belong here'.

A 'culturally rich environment' is predicated, primarily, on three things:

1. Culture and sub-culture: 'You can have the same type of people, in the same place, at the same time, doing the same thing, and they will still think and behave completely differently unless they are "controlled" by the social norms and boundaries that you set.'
2. Ethics: Refers to well-founded standards of right and wrong that prescribe what our employees ought to do, usually in terms of rights, obligations, benefits, fairness, or specific virtues. But different cultures have different ideas of what 'ethics' look like, so what does our organisational moral compass look like? Is it truly inclusive?
3. Trust: The firm belief in the reliability, truth, or ability of someone, or something, to be good and honest and to do no harm: for example, the trust the public place in the NHS that it will heal, not harm, patients; or that our moral compass ensures that justice is not only done, but is seen to be done.

If you can get all of that right, hope increases exponentially. Why? Because staff see a noble vision and not a grand illusion, but this involves having 'the right people, in the right place, at the right time, doing the right thing, *being led by the right people*'.

Conclusion

The only way to tackle a toxic organisation is to be proactive as soon as you identify the problem. You must attack the causes and build a 'culturally rich environment' where toxicity cannot thrive, and this will, necessarily, involve 'kissing the frog'. It is only after that difficult transparent reckoning that reformed organisations will be able to develop a clear vision with a moral compass, not just a list of facile values.

Notes

1. https://www.theguardian.com/business/2013/nov/23/coop-scandal-paul-flowers-mutual-societies
2. https://www.theguardian.com/business/2013/nov/23/coop-scandal-paul-flowers-mutual-societies
3. https://www.oxfordreference.com/view/10.1093/acref/9780191843730.001.0001/q-oro-ed5-00007298
4. gov.uk/government/statistics/tribunal-statistics-quarterly-april-to-june-2020
5. https://www.business-live.co.uk/retail-consumer/former-post-office-ceo-paula-20465662
6. https://www.lawgazette.co.uk/news/post-office-attacked-and-disparaged-sub-postmasters-judge-finds/5102542.article
7. https://www.computerweekly.com/news/252476160/Call-for-former-Post-Office-CEO-to-step-down-from-public-roles-after-IT-court-battle-lost
8. https://www.thetimes.co.uk/article/should-those-who-sent-the-sub-postmasters-to-prison-now-face-court-themselves-srdp8kjn6
9. https://assets.publishing.service.gov.uk/government/uploads/system/uploads/attachment_data/file/407209/KL_lessons_learned_report_FINAL.pdf
10. https://www.managementtoday.co.uk/greg-dyke-leadership-stories-told-you/article/935797
11. https://www.thesun.co.uk/news/16639274/tories-boris-johnson-u-turn-sleaze-mp-owen-paterson/
12. https://transleadership.com/wp-content/uploads/ToxicLeadership.pdf

CHAPTER 3

Resisting the silence of the cabal: resorting to social and alternative media

Pat Harvey

Accordingto the *Summary Report on the Findings from the Scoping and Information Gathering Phase* of work commissioned from the consultants Korn Ferry, the British Psychological Society wishes to be 'relevant', 'desirable', 'sustainable', and 'agile'. From their contacts with members of the Society in late 2020, Korn Ferry identified 'connectivity and connection to everything the Society does' to be of central importance to members. However, they discovered that members who were active within the various networks complained of slowness, errors, 'over censorship', and editing of communications. The *Summary Report* states:

> Communication is the biggest single issue for member networks … This restriction around communication was perceived to be the result of the Society's risk aversion … Those that we spoke to expressed a view that the Staff tries to control and vet all communications as a means of managing risk and that this leads to those leading the Networks to feel an inherent distrust.

During 2020, throughout the Covid-19 disruptions, some BPS members who had a range of disparate dissatisfactions about the functioning of the Society began to form a loose network. This happened initially via telephone contacts between members who knew each other, or knew of each other, and who were concerned about specific problems in their current relationship with the BPS. This might have begun as a concern with the way in which a topic was being debated (or not debated). It then became a frustration and growing objection to the way in which the BPS responded to their efforts to pursue these concerns, or it had just ignored them, provoking instant anger in the wake of being disrespected.

The telephone contacts progressed into email threads. Some were copied more widely to other members, who would otherwise not have known each other. What they all shared was a sense of frustration with those running the Society. The emails described a pattern of queries to senior managers going unanswered or being quickly blocked. Members were treated with hostility, there was poor consultation with interested parties about policy-sensitive matters, a lack of meaningful or useful information on the Society website, and evidence of censorship by *The Psychologist* and other Society publications.

A multiplicity of email threads rapidly became tangled and inboxes were overloaded. Significant energy was generated by linking up and discussing how poorly the Society seemed able to deal with dissent of any kind. However, networks of this kind have no obvious strategic focus or ability to communicate directly to 67,000 members or any wider interested public. Using BPS structures or its website were clearly not options. Nor did the Society's publication *The Psychologist*, despite its stated claims, seem to be functioning to *allow*, let alone assist, communication from ordinary members, though it obediently acted as a noticeboard for the BPS leadership.

BPSWatch.com was set up as a WordPress blog in November 2020, to be run by three named members of the BPS[1] with an associated Twitter account FakeBPSCommentary, @psychsocwatchuk[2] monitored and run on a daily basis by this author. The stories of these alternative media and how they have fared will be told below. However, it is important to set these in the context of the limitations of the orthodox forms of BPS information/communication, most notably of the limitations of the widely circulated *The Psychologist* magazine.

The Psychologist, its role, and its failings

In March 2021, *The Psychologist* and Digest Editorial Advisory Committee published a document, *The Psychologist Policies and Protocols*.[3] This was typical of many BPS documents, where the authorship and membership ratification are not clear.[4] The following is relevant for our purposes, as it constitutes the publication's mission statement:

3. The Psychologist's policy

3.1 The Psychologist will be a publication that diffuses and advances a knowledge of psychology pure and applied:

- for members, it will contain information and knowledge relevant to the discipline and profession of psychology;
- for non-members, it will provide a taste of what psychology is and what psychologists do;
- for potential members, it will provide a contemporary and dynamic image of a profession worth joining and of a Society that offers significant membership services; and
- for the media, it will encourage media awareness of information that is of value and relevance to the general public.

3.2 The Psychologist will fulfil various roles within the Society:

- as a forum for the exchange of views, the discussion of issues, and exploring controversy, sometimes across issues as well as within an issue where possible/appropriate;
- as a source of information about the views of the Society;
- as a place to publish Society news and business, and to reflect the Society's member-voted policy themes and current priorities; and
- as a link to other sources of information such as the Society website.

The phrase 'all things to all people' may well come to mind at this point, regarding the stated or rhetorical role and function of *The Psychologist*. The many concerns about specific psychological topics, how these are being covered or not covered, issues of professional practice, reports on how the Society is responding and how the Society is governed/governs itself are surely a remit far too wide for such a 'magazine'. However, that is exactly what it has claimed for itself since 1988, when it 'emerged from the *Bulletin of the British Psychological Society*'.[5] The late J. Richard Marshall, BPS member and critical psychologist, in personal communications at the time, was sceptical. He predicted that this revamping would create a magazine in which critical thought and intellectual rigour would be eclipsed by a superficial public relations exercise for the discipline and its contemporary leaders. Richard's prediction was accurate.

Even given the inherent problems of a claimed role and remit that is too wide, and the contradictions of purported independence from what is clearly in every respect its parent body, *The Psychologist* has exceeded all forebodings. In recent times, it has failed to reflect balanced discussion in its choice of coverage of contentious topics. The editor has been reluctant to print letters complaining of that lack of balance. Critical comments placed below articles online have been removed by the editor. The content has failed to inform members of even the most basic facts of the Society's ongoing governance and recent financial oversight failures. The organisational crisis outlined in Chapter 1 was not reported, leaving the members either in a state of ignorance or gleaning fragments of information from newspapers and informal communications with more informed colleagues.

Tangling with *The Psychologist*

By May 2021, we witnessed a catalogue of criticisms of *The Psychologist*'s coverage and its failure to inform members of serious matters of concern within the Society. Taking one example, I had conducted a tetchy exchange with the editor back in December 2020 about a decision to solicit, and publish, deliberately what was very clearly a hostile and very one-sided polemic about the outcome of an important UK judicial review.[6] Having expressed this in the comments section, beneath the online version, the editor responded thus:

> The editorial team approached Reubs Walsh at the beginning of the year, originally about writing (on a voluntary basis) on gender

diversity and autism. Inevitably as the legal case developed, that became more of a focus, and as we had the article ready to go (with some amends once the outcome was known), that seemed a good time to put it on the website. Part of a magazine's role is to be topical, particularly with its online presence. All readers are free to agree with the article (many have), disagree with it, ignore it, as they choose. We will continue to provide that forum for discussion and debate and will not be stifled by any responsibility to side with a particular position ... The 'truth' is not always so simple, and the 'law' can be questioned.

Note that this piece from a trans activist, Reubs Walsh, who was not a BPS member, had been carefully prepared over months with editorial help and polishing. It reflected a highly partisan view, and the editor offered no alternative account to the readership. The piece could only serve to exacerbate clinicians' anxiety about their current legal duty and ethical responsibility. It would add to the confusion generated by existing problems with the Society's guidelines on the subject and the ambiguity around their applicability to children and young people. The editor had uncritically printed, at the foot of a letter, not even an article, the Society's retrospective disclaimer: a questionable assertion that the guidelines had been intended for adults only.[7] This remains questionable because there is a specific section within the guidelines concerning young people and their future 'reproductive options'.

At that stage, the guidelines had not been amended to carry that 'health warning—adults only' for practitioners. Moreover, unless practitioners stumbled across that one brief note at the foot of a letter in *The Psychologist*, they would still be operating on recommendations regarding the content of counselling to minors which remained within the document, and which would be deemed legally fraught by that judicial review. Only following my protracted complaints process with the Society is the rider 'for adults only' now belatedly part of those guidelines. *The Psychologist* had actively played a dubious, even irresponsible, role in this very complex matter, and this is merely one of a number of examples. I pick up this unresolved debacle about the Gender Guidelines in Chapter 4.

Tackling the editorial board

I had separately, in common with a number of others, been invited by the editor to complain to the chair of the Digest/editorial board of *The Psychologist* if I was not satisfied with his responses. By May 2021, I felt there was much of serious substance to complain about. The most important immediate news was that the president elect, Nigel MacLennan, elected by members on an explicit mandate to reform BPS governance, had been removed from office and expelled from the Society.

The immediate concern, and for many of us shocked reaction, was that the expulsion had been announced 'out of the blue' and without any framing context, via direct communications to members from the Society. It was also accompanied by the making and propagation of a YouTube video.

The Psychologist had immediately covered this and posted the link to the video.[8] I wrote to the chair of the Editorial Board (full correspondence below[9]), stating:

> The video goes way beyond an announcement to members and the public that he has been expelled from the BPS and details allegations IN ADVANCE OF his rightful appeal. No other media publication would have done this, their legal departments would have told them that whilst they could report the fact of an expulsion pending an appeal, the details would have been curtailed by the principle of sub judice.

The chair's immediate reply[10] acknowledged: 'Given that *The Psychologist* has a much wider audience, Jon reflected that it's [sic] inclusion in the piece "The Society is at a Crossroads" was not appropriate. On that basis the video has been removed.'

The allusion to 'Jon' is to Jon Sutton, the editor of *The Psychologist*. My email had also raised a number of other concerns, one being that the vice president Dr David Murphy's recent resignation had been reported by *The Psychologist*. However, Murphy had protested on Twitter that the publication had so misrepresented/failed to cover the reasons for the resignation that he felt impelled to post a screenshot of the whole of his actual resignation letter.[11] The contents were a bombshell, and they have received detailed coverage in the mainstream media (see below), but not in *The Psychologist*.

The Psychologist as a poor source
of information about the BPS

Just how poorly *The Psychologist* had been performing its rhetorically expressed role during a growing crisis at the Society is illustrated by the fact that the BPS had, by May 2021, lost its whole presidential team (two resignations and an expulsion). Also, the chief executive officer had been suspended since November, the chief finance officer had resigned, and there was an ongoing police investigation into an alleged large fraud.

By now, the members should surely also have also been informed that the National Council for Voluntary Organisations (NCVO), called in by the BPS to advise on strategic direction, had withdrawn. The NCVO were so perturbed by the culture and governance failings they found within the Society that their staff had requested to cease their involvement. The NCVO believed it would be 'inappropriate to place BPS staff and volunteers in a situation that risks causing psychological and emotional harm'.

This was an ironic and deeply distasteful verdict about, note, a *Psychological* Society. This event was left to us and the mainstream media to report to members; there was radio silence in *The Psychologist*. Had we not publicised our case and the mass media had not picked up the story, the membership would have remained in the dark about the serious concerns held by the NCVO about the toxic culture of the BPS. In a parallel process of covering up important information, *The Psychologist* failed to report that the Charity Commission regulators had been called in to examine poor governance in the Society. Again, the membership would be oblivious to this engagement had we not alerted them, alongside the mainstream media (see below).

There is little sign that *The Psychologist* and its supervisory board will exercise any radical changes of approach to informing members. In their own words, 'the committee were satisfied that the editor's independence has been maintained—the magazine is not being silenced'.[12] If that is the case, we are saddled, for the time being at least, with an extraordinarily incurious editorial ethos. Furthermore, the following endnote from the editor demonstrates a reluctance to engage with the members:

> P.S. Comment is disabled on this post; I feel for very good reason given past experience. This is an opportunity to explain our

position, rather than an invitation to debate. However, email addresses are there for both the Chair of PDEAC and myself, and any letters for publication will be considered in the usual way.

At the time of writing, the editor, Jon Sutton, has once again turned down a letter from me for publication, this one a plea for clarification of much ongoing concern identified by both the former vice president and president elect, about the £6 million 'Change Programme'. Sutton prevaricated about its publication and then refused, *without giving reasons*, and decided it should be redirected to the Change Programme director (the latter was acting as CEO, during the period of suspension of Sarb Bajwa).

This illustrates a frequent tactic of funnelling an important matter into a narrow backroom sphere, rather than allowing it into the public domain. Put simply, *The Psychologist* has played a key role in protecting the leadership of the BPS and blocking open debate in the membership about serious matters of concern. The silencing of those asking awkward questions for the BPS leadership is a price being readily paid by the editor and defended by those allegedly scrutinising its judgements.

This scenario afforded the emergence of activity designed to compensate for this inadequate approach from *The Psychologist*, which I now describe. Sutton had chosen recurrently to avoid any reporting of the crisis that he and others at the centre of the organisation knew full well was present and serious. To their shame, his editorial advisors were complicit in this denial of information to the membership. This created a political opportunity and moral necessity for others to fill that silence.

Alternative information sources: setting up the blog and Twitter

The BPSWatch blog

The Covid-19 summer of 2020 had seen escalating concerns being expressed by members. Unanswered phone calls and emails were increasingly the norm, according to many complainants we knew, and we trusted their accounts. 'Covid' was to become a new cover story for poor responsiveness from 'the BPS'. I happened to say in frustration to David Pilgrim in a call, 'Maybe we need a blog—what are members even paying for?' His enthusiastic response then led to the corralling of Peter Harvey, who shares a study at home with me, and had the technical skills and patience, to become a blog administrator.

The three of us running the blog share commonalities: we are all retired or semi-retired and have all had long careers in psychology and as psychology service managers in the NHS. We have all held elected office (in the Division of Clinical Psychology and the History and Philosophy Section). We shared a growing alarm at what we had discovered to be happening to the BPS, but wished to see it restored to health, not destroyed. In that respect, we saw ourselves as 'critical friends'. Our past experience, plus our lack of vulnerability to career damage, provided us with an unusual opportunity, and, we thought, obligation, to speak out.

The new bloggers had from the outset built up a wider network of regular contacts amongst concerned members, but none of us had known the president elect prior to considering publishing a blog. We made contact with him and became aware of his agenda for reform and his experiences of resistance to this from senior staff and volunteer office holders. These discussions soon helped us to understand that there were, inherent in the Society, deep structural governance and resulting procedural problems. These often culminated in a lack of openness and transparency.

We soon realised that there was an 'information blackout' about serious matters. The BPS has a director of communications and engagement, and the 'comms team' issued specific written directives as to how questions should be fielded or passed on to the team to handle. In our opinion, this was put in place to shut down communication, not to enhance it, and illustrates perfectly the criticisms from members, heard by Korn Ferry, of the actions of staff reported in the opening paragraph of this chapter. We believed that this blackout strategy was impacting directly upon membership democracy and, ultimately, upon public protection.

Threat of legal action

The opening blog post on BPSWatch.com written by me[13] on 20 November 2020, and the second post by David Pilgrim,[14] originally referred to an alleged fraud at the Society, and to the *fact* of the suspension of the Society's CEO and finance director. It also reported the involvement of the Charity Commission, from whom I had personally received a communication stating:

> We are currently engaging with the Society over a number of issues and have found deficiencies in some areas of operation. Whilst I would expect the charity to have a robust and well managed complaints process, this may have not been the case in the past.

Within ten days, we received from the director of legal and governance at the BPS 'cease and desist' instructions, which carried the threat of legal action against us for defamation. In a state of legal uncertainty (we were ordinary members with no access at this stage to immediate legal advice), we opted to remove these references, with the exception of those to the Charity Commission. We have subsequently come to understand how naivety about the implications of verbal imprecision can leave the unwary vulnerable to threats of legal action, from those in power at the BPS.

There remained facts which we believed, then and now, that the membership had every right to know, and which have eventually been confirmed in the public domain. These facts all impacted directly upon the functioning of the BPS. The CEO *was* suspended, even if the actual details and some other matters rightly should have been kept confidential. However, the *material fact* of his suspension continued to be euphemised in correspondence from the BPS in terms such as 'extended leave'. There was also the alleged fraud being investigated by Leicestershire Police over a significantly longer period of time and then still ongoing. That material fact was finally admitted in the Trustees Report[15] to the 2021 AGM, although the BPS were not so careful to use the word 'alleged' as we have done. This may be because those presenting the accounts had to provide a public explanation for the many thousands of pounds missing.

Nowhere does there appear to be any open acknowledgement of the nature of the ongoing engagement of the regulatory body, the Charity Commission. This has not reached the end point of a full formal statutory inquiry to date. However, it remains the case that the Society is being held subject to statutory directives related to legal compliance and objective-setting, and there is ongoing scrutiny from the Commission. This was euphemised as follows:

> It is clear to us that stronger governance processes will be required in the future, and this work is well underway. We have kept the Charity Commission fully informed of developments throughout and continue to engage with them.[16]

Members who had not been following our alternative media posts about the Charity Commission may have been surprised to discover they were involved *at all* when a 'Charity Commission probe' was reported in *The Daily Telegraph*.[17] The BPS chose to chide and dismiss both the newspaper and us (by now referred to at BPS HQ as 'the Malcontents') as follows:

> We are disappointed that the Daily Telegraph has chosen to repeat the views of a small minority of BPS members who are unwilling to accept the outcome of our consultations and policy positions.

By now, we had come to recognise a favoured defence: 'Problem? What problem?'

The blog content

Visitors to the BPSWatch.com blog would find that by the summer of 2022, there had been over fifty substantive subject posts in a year. Most, but not all, posts were authored by the three bloggers, David Pilgrim, Peter Harvey, and me, augmented by pieces from Ashley Conway and David Marks, alongside some anonymised posts. The latter are few in number because we opted to model transparency for the BPS and our commitment to freedom of expression.

The subjects have been categorised by the administrator under the headings below (the number in each category adds up to more than fifty-two because some posts are placed in more than one category for ease of navigation).

Governance	25
Financial issues	6
Board of Trustees	10
Expulsion of the president elect	14
The Psychologist	8
Academic freedom and censorship	5
Memory and law groups	9
'False memory syndrome'	5
Ethics	3
Prescribing rights	2
IAPT	4
Uncategorised	4

Whilst there are, at the point of writing, only thirty-four registered followers, the viewing rate of posts is high and peaks as each new post is signalled on Twitter (see below).

In the period 20 November to 31 December 2020, there were 6,577 views by 3,004 visitors.

In the period 1 January to 13 October 2021, there were 24,256 views by 10,277 visitors.

With this empirical picture of a year's activity on the blog in mind, I now turn to my Twitter account.

The Twitter account: @psychsocwatch

The decision to set up the blog necessitated consideration of how to publicise it. I surmised that the best option was to open a dedicated Twitter account. Neither of the two other bloggers had an account, and they expressed a strong resistance to any personal involvement, being wary of the dubious reputation of Twitter, for its poor quality of debate and negative emotional climate. Hence the account became very largely my responsibility. The immediacy of Twitter meant that it might alert the membership to ongoing events. These would include links to newspaper articles that reported the turbulent events within the Society and reminders of ongoing key problems and events, about which they were not being informed.

Initial hiccoughs: permanent suspension of the first Twitter account

The first iteration of the Twitter account was titled BPSWatch@watch-bps. A complaint was lodged quickly with Twitter that we were *impersonating* the BPS. (*Impersonation* is one of a number of breaches of Twitter rules.) I was instructed to change the name. The account then became ScrutinisingtheBPS@WatchBPS, so named, I thought, to sufficiently demonstrate no intent to impersonate the BPS. A further complaint of impersonating the BPS was made and upheld, resulting in a permanent suspension of that account and its source details, which has not been lifted despite appeal.

Why were we accused and then found guilty of 'impersonating the BPS' by Twitter HQ? One cannot discuss this sort of basic question with a real person. However, Twitter provides its users with three terms that signify that so-called parody accounts are not intending to impersonate. Hence our new account could be created via other identification details to use two of those three terms. This is the reason for its odd styling as FakeBPSCommentary@psychsocwatchuk.

I have followed only seven other accounts, in order to reduce my timeline content and focus on the matters of specific interest, but I followed at the beginning *The Psychologist*'s Twitter, @psychmag. Our account was eventually blocked, I believe, for objecting to a highly partisan tweet supporting the England football team on @psychmag—which seemed to me to be something of a personal misuse of the forum. After all, the Society is UK-wide (the clue is in the word 'British') and supposed to be an official account for professional forum. It is not the English Psychological Society or a football forum, and yet here is what the 'magazine' averred in its tweet:

> The Psychologist @psychmag 29 Jun
> We're in the 'easy' half of the draw …
> Germany didn't look that good against Hungary …
> Harry Kane will surely hit form at some point …
> It's coming home …
> thepsychologist.bps.org.uk/its-coming-home #ENG

This was a rather petulant and pointless, thin-skinned response to block us, since screenshots allow for other accounts to visit the site and send us relevant material for our Twitter. It does, of course, reinforce the criticisms we have been making and which ultimately prompts the question, 'What should *The Psychologist* be?' Is it a serious attempt at academic journalism and an inclusive forum for professional debate, or is it just a safe, restricted, and conservative noticeboard for those running the BPS? Our answer, as is clear episodically in this book, is clear. The magazine functions to defend the employer of the editor, promote 'good news' about psychology, and suppress serious debate.

Twitter activity

I tweeted 881 individual tweets in the period 20 November 2020 to 13 October 2021. These made 1,248,000 impressions (impressions being the number of times people have actually seen the tweet on Twitter itself).

In terms of tweet content, all tweets were focused upon subject matter concerning the BPS, directly or indirectly, and were intended to inform. They alerted followers, at the time 925, and potentially a range of others, via tweets, retweets, and quote tweets, to matters they might otherwise not have known about. These included new blog posts, posts by others, mainstream media articles on the BPS dysfunction (a partial list of those is below), and other internal affairs not being reported by the BPS or *The Psychologist*.

Utilising the Twitter format

As has been acknowledged elsewhere:

> Getting your message across in a clear and concise manner always helps keep your social media audience interested but becomes essential on Twitter. When you only have 140 characters in which to fit your message, every single one of them counts.

As the most immediate and 'telegraphic' means of communicating, Twitter does not allow for nuanced argument, but can effectively capture interest and signal important information elsewhere by providing links, images, and screenshots. Single words or acronyms can be used that refer to circumstances and tactics at the BPS, which we have been highlighting and critiquing. 'Cabal' or 'oligarchy', for example, has become our way of referring to the current regime, and DARVO (deny, attack, and reverse victim and offender) to describe the process now invoked when a member persists with a concern. They are accused of bullying and harassing officers and threatened with disciplinary action.

I learned that tweets which contain an image receive more attention, so where possible, these were added. Changes in the imagery of the banner heading of the page were made at regular intervals, often reflecting a particular current concern (such as the YouTube video issued by the BPS about the expelled president elect).

From early 2021, we began to contact and discuss the 'BPS crisis' with individual journalists in the mainstream media, and our Twitter account continues at the point of writing to be followed by some of them.

Mainstream media interest

There have been a number of articles on the BPS crisis since the beginning of 2021. Most have been in a publication called *Third Sector*. This covers voluntary sector news and jobs including charity finance, fundraising, governance, management, and communications, which acts as a 'feeder' of the most interesting subject matter to the newspapers. There have also been articles in *The Daily Telegraph* and *The Times* newspapers. Since the reader may be dissuaded by the paywall, these were the headlines as they appeared during 2021:

> 'Long-standing British Psychological Society trustee quits citing governance and spending concerns'—*Third Sector*, 11 February 2021[18]

> 'British Psychological Society president steps down'—*Third Sector*, 15 April 2021[19]

> 'Exclusive: British Psychological Society faces Charity Commission probe'—*The Telegraph*, 25 April 2021[20]

'British Psychological Society expels president-elect amid claims of "persistent bullying"'—*Third Sector*, 6 May 2021[21]

'Psychological society president ousted for alleged bullying'—*The Times*, 7 May 2021[22]

'NCVO pulled out of consultancy work with charity amid fears it would be "detrimental" to its staff'—*Third Sector*, 21 June 2021[23]

In addition to contacts with the mainstream media, we have also made links with other alternative media groups including CBTWatch, Charity Sanity, and Locked up Living. In line with the remit of the latter's focus upon dysfunctional organisations, it gave us airtime for a lengthy podcast.[24]

What might we have achieved to date?

This is what I have learned from running this account. Running a Twitter page, such as @psychsocwatchuk, can take over your life, indeed, become a way of life, as people engaged in similar projects will confirm. There is an insistent internal imperative to keep checking your phone in order not to 'miss' anything. Clearly, this is set in the wider context of the virtual social lives that increasing numbers of people live on various forms of social media, sometimes to the detriment of 'real' social life. The underlying concerns we had about the demise of our learned and professional body are by no means resolved at this time. They continue to energise our focus, which has become a significant and time-consuming part of our daily lives and interactions around the blog and Twitter.

The British Psychological Society remains in the grip of the structural and personnel problems that have led it to this low point. It is still beset by the inherent contradictions within the wide range of its 'mission', or more accurately, its 'missions'. Other psychology societies worldwide have the same particular tensions between their academic and applied wings, burgeoning bureaucracy, and marketisation. I have noticed, and now become tuned in to, how many other organisations are being described as having similar problems to the BPS, from the

National Trust to the Vegan Society. It is also evident that whistleblowers are still suffering significant personal harm, which suggests a wider cultural problem of deceit and unaccountable power in our culture. The matter of 'bullshit' in modern life is picked up in Chapter 7. The specific betrayal of academic values by the BPS is considered in Chapter 8.

Have we achieved anything at all with over fifty blog posts, and the more than 800 somewhat niche tweets, which have been viewed well over a million times? Can any of the changes now being proposed to the shambolic complaints procedure, for example, be ascribed to pressure we have brought to bear? Is the BPS any nearer to an independent, free of conflict-of-interest governance structure than it was when we began the alternative media project? We are too close in time to answer these pertinent questions, so here are a few preliminary thoughts.

Members regularly contact us to tell us to 'keep up the work' and give us examples where the impact of our information has informed discussions at various meetings. Beyond that, and in the absence of concrete radical reform at this stage, the question of the extent of our impact, or lack thereof, may well be left for future historians of the Society to consider.

Healthy changes will surely rely upon greater engagement of the wider membership. Thanks to us, a small section of that membership is at least better informed than it was. Our Twitter account has less than 1,000 identified followers, not all members, but it is clear from the numbers seeing the tweets that far more people check in regularly. This is confirmed by numerous conversations where early, and particularly mid-career, psychologists who share our concerns indicate that they wish to keep a low profile for the various reasons which make them feel vulnerable and insecure about speaking out.

One issue is that contentious psychological questions form the meat of much of identity politics, and these days being associated with those debates feels too personally and professionally risky. It is also a matter of interest, but not surprise, that we are told that we are closely followed by key individuals *within* the BPS, although they do not respond to us in any way on the various forums.

We have fielded numerous phone calls from other unhappy individuals, members, ex-members, and non-members, who are having poor experiences of the BPS, the Charity Commission, and some aggressive groups of activists. Two of us have fairly extensive forensic experience, on an individual and organisational level, so we are not prey to the dangers of uncritical listening. Nor are we in the business of supporting any one side of contentious debates, even sides with which we personally agree.

Our central interest is in dysfunctional processes (the misgovernance in the BPS), not in riding one particular hobby-horse. This foregrounding of misgovernance when alluding to illustrative content is evident in most of the other chapters in the book and in blog posts on BPSWatch.com.

As my most recent blog post[25] made clear, our interest is in seeing the Society healthy and thriving. In failing its members, the British Psychological Society is ultimately failing the public. The important yardstick by which any reforms the Society makes must be evaluated ultimately relate to the value of psychology to society. A radically reformed British Psychological Society needs governance structures that reduce cronyism, encourage wider member engagement, and which open up healthy debates. The BPS must change drastically in order to support psychology's best contribution to the world outside itself, surely the major reason for its existence. Whether or not the Society is now capable of surviving is a moot point, to which I return at the end of Chapter 8.

Notes

1. https://bpswatch.com/about
2. @psychsocwatch UK: 'Pat Harvey on behalf of http://BPSWatch.com blog. Alternative media means of finding out about #BadBPS. Contact us on BPSWatch@btinternet.com #evidencebasedtweets.'
3. https://thepsychologist.bps.org.uk/sites/thepsychologist.bps.org.uk/files/files/psychologistpolicyjun2021.pdf
4. This may seem like a nit-picking point, but for a situation where there are ongoing and sometimes radical alterations to policy documents and guidelines over the years, it is important that the origins of political and policy stances are owned by individuals acting on behalf of the Society. Only then will those with an interest in historical developments accessing Society archives be able to see where and who ideas came from. Historians must be able to trace provenance, within their focus. When the focus is one of organisational

dysfunction, then access to evidence of provenance is a centrally important matter. This point is picked up in Chapter 9 by Ashley Conway.

5. https://thepsychologist.bps.org.uk/volume-34/september-2021/psychologist-and-digest-editorial-advisory-committee
6. https://thepsychologist.bps.org.uk/blow-rights-transgender-children
7. https://thepsychologist.bps.org.uk/volume-33/october-2020/freedom-expression-around-diversity-guidelines
8. https://thepsychologist.bps.org.uk/volume-34/june-2021/society-crossroads

9. Dear Dr Stephens

    I write to you (27 May 2021) in your capacity as Chair of *The Psychologist* and Digest Policy Committee. Since last year I have had a number of concerns about the content of *The Psychologist* and the attitude and stated position of the Editor when I have raised these concerns.

    My reason for writing to your editorial board at this point, however, is to raise a specific formal objection to the fact that *The Psychologist* has published, on behalf of the BPS, a YouTube video, https://www.youtube.com/watch?v=gGqRl1Rot1k which is clearly highly damaging to an individual, to his reputation, his livelihood and his mental well-being. The video goes way beyond an announcement to members and the public that he has been expelled from the BPS and details allegations IN ADVANCE OF his rightful appeal. No other media publication would have done this, their legal departments would have told them that whilst they could report the **fact** of an expulsion pending an appeal, the **details** would have been curtailed by the principle of *sub judice*. Please also note that, regarding the content of the accompanying print statement from the BPS, the former Vice President who resigned in February has also protested:

    David Murphy, 2019–20 BPS President @ClinPsychDavid May 19

    I was disappointed to read the statement in @psychmag today https://thepsychologist.bps.org.uk/volume-34/june-2021/society-crossroads … which states that I 'chose to resign' without any mention of the reasons. The subsequent focus on gender & prescribing issues may imply these were involved, I've posted my resignation letter below https://twitter.com/ClinPsychDavid/status/1394985946446184450?s=20

    In neither case, it would seem, has the Editor or his staff sought to obtain/print a response from the individuals as would be the normal practice in a media report of a controversy, or to give any contextual comment. Further, in relation to the '...turbulent year...' referred to in the BPS statement, *The Psychologist* has published **not one** item covering this '...turbulence...'. How is that acting to inform members? The publication of the YouTube video is particularly culpable of your editor (and your board if they were consulted) since, when I have raised the issues of duty to members, balance and editorial independence of any current regime at the BPS on other matters, these are the kind of responses that I have received: https://thepsychologist.bps.org.uk/blow-rights-transgender-children comments section.

Jon Sutton 1 on Sat, 12/12/2020—11:52

We are not a 'house journal', we are a magazine. Our responsibility is not to speak for the Society or to align with any documents it might publish; it is to provide a forum for communication, discussion and controversy among members and beyond.

When I challenged this:

Patricia Harvey on Sat, 12/12/2020—16:05

I regret that the editor's response 'we are a magazine' diverts from the very serious comments I have made about responsibility to members.

When is a magazine rather more than a magazine? Maybe when it is 'the official monthly publication of The British Psychological Society', https://www.bps.org.uk/about-psychologist

I had asked for a retraction of a misleading statement that *The Psychologist* had printed on behalf of the Society and so I added

I note that *The Psychologist* is not listed as a magazine signed up to IPSO, so I am unable to report to them that it has printed a statement from the Society that is patently false—in order to attempt to secure a retraction in print and online.

Jon Sutton replied:

... and just to add, I'll look into IPSO membership, thanks for the tip.

When I followed up the IPSO issue. I got this response:

On IPSO, yes I've been in touch with them about membership and the associated costs. I wouldn't expect immediate movement on that, because we've got a real job on our hands simply getting the issues out in the current circumstances.

What does 'immediate movement' mean? It is hardly a significant task to ask for the funding and join. Especially when the BPS is stumping up £6million for the so-called Change Project, and application would be a few minutes online. Had *The Psychologist* signed up to IPSO there are three other matters of important inaccuracies that I would have reported to them having had no satisfactory response from the Editor, who has several times told me if I wasn't happy to report it to the Board.

On this matter of the video, therefore, I am reporting it to you and the board as I believe that it constitutes actual targeted harassment. I am also of the opinion that it might be in breach of the BPS Code of Ethics and Conduct and the Member Conduct Rules.

Yours sincerely
Pat Harvey AFBPsS CPsychol

10. Dear Pat

    Thanks for your letter and for raising these concerns. I plan to table these for discussion at the next meeting of *The Psychologist* and Digest Editorial Advisory Committee on 24th June. I felt that your first raised point warranted some urgency of response so I discussed it today with our editor, Jon Sutton. Jon's view was that while the video featuring Professor Carol McGuinness as Interim Chair of the Board of Trustee has been widely disseminated among BPS members, it is unlisted on YouTube. Given that *The Psychologist* has a much wider audience, Jon reflected that it's [sic] inclusion in the piece 'The Society is at a crossroads' was not appropriate. On that basis the video has been removed. I will feedback in due course following our meeting on the 24th. Thanks again for drawing these matters to my attention.

    Best Wishes,
    Richard.

11. 'I was disappointed to read the statement in @psychmag today https://thepsychologist.bps.org.uk/volume-34/june-2021/society-crossroads… which states that I "chose to resign" without any mention of the reasons. The subsequent focus on gender & prescribing issues may imply these were involved, I've posted my resignation letter below' https://twitter.com/ClinPsychDavid/status/1394985946446184450?s=20

12. https://thepsychologist.bps.org.uk/volume-34/september-2021/psychologist-and-digest-editorial-advisory-committee

13. https://bpswatch.com/2020/11/20/why-the-blog-and-why-now

14. The Mess We Are In' https://bpswatch.com/2020/11/26/195

15. www.bps.org.uk/sites/www.bps.org.uk/files/Annual%20Reports/Reviews/Trustees%20Annual%20Report%202020.pdf

16. www.bps.org.uk/news-and-policy/bps-response-article-daily-telegraph

17. www.telegraph.co.uk/news/2021/04/25/exclusive-british-psychological-society-faces-charity-commission

18. www.thirdsector.co.uk/long-standing-british-psychological-society-trustee-quits-citing-governance-spending-concerns/governance/article/1707182

19. www.thirdsector.co.uk/british-psychological-society-president-steps-down/article/1712903

20. www.telegraph.co.uk/news/2021/04/25/exclusive-british-psychological-society-faces-charity-commission

21. www.thirdsector.co.uk/british-psychological-society-expels-president-elect-amid-claims-persistent-bullying/governance/article/1714936

22. www.thetimes.co.uk/article/psychological-society-president-ousted-for-alleged-bullying-pfwdx8cm6

23. www.thirdsector.co.uk/ncvo-pulled-consultancy-work-charity-amid-fears-detrimental-its-staff/management/article/1719976

24. https://open.spotify.com/episode/07SFd7dlwGLs9zPYS7duWl?si=RuJpKHRcQbSBWVSY5gT8jg&dl_branch=1&nd=1

25. https://bpswatch.com/2021/09/19/the-british-psychological-society-failing-the-public

CHAPTER 4

Policy capture at the BPS (1): the Gender Guidelines

Pat Harvey

T he dysfunctional governance and operation of the British Psychological Society supports a culture of cronyism and capture. An 'in-group' of serial office-holders amongst members, working with head office staff, encourage 'ideological party lines' to develop, at times, about controversial policies. Determined activists can, with a continuing presence within committees, pursue their goals successfully, thereby excluding a democratic inclusion of diverse views across the Society's membership. A key example of this is the manner in which transgender ideology has permeated BPS policy, via their *Guidelines on Gender Sexuality and Relationship Diversity* (for brevity henceforth, the 'Guidelines').

'Transgender' denotes, or relates to, a person whose sense of identity and gender does not correspond with their birth sex. An ideology has been formed around the increasing numbers of persons identifying as transgender, which focuses not only upon legal status and rights but also upon designating gender as superordinate to biological sex.

This chapter begins by introducing the Guidelines before discussing the process of their creation. Detailed attention will then be given to the form the Guidelines have taken, their content and the tone of their strictures and prescriptions. My intention is to illustrate the impact of ideological capture within the BPS, in this particular case. (Another example is offered in Chapter 5 by Ashley Conway.) Reference will be made to the contrast with another current set of BPS professional guidelines (on autism), which more properly represent what is expected from a scientific and professional body. Finally, the chapter will recount some of the opposition to the Guidelines within the BPS.

Introduction to the Guidelines

The Guidelines were published in 2019[1] and are introduced on the BPS website for download as follows:

> These guidelines relate to gender, sexuality and relationship diverse (GSRD) adults and young people (aged 18 years and over).
>
> That is, broadly people who do not identify as heterosexual, monogamous or cisgender.
>
> This includes lesbian, gay, bisexual and transgender (LGBT) people as well as people who identify as asexual (do not or rarely experience sexual attraction), are agender (have no gender), have a non-binary gender (have a gender other than male or female), are pansexual (have attraction irrespective of gender), and many other groups.
>
> The guidelines do not, however, relate to anything non-consensual.
>
> The identities and practices considered here are not in themselves pathological and are part of human diversity.
>
> These guidelines are aimed at applied psychologists working with mental distress, but may also be applied in associated psychological fields.
>
> The principles they are based upon are derived from both the literature and best practice agreement of experts in the field and may also be applied to other disciplines, such as counselling, psychotherapy, psychiatry, medicine, nursing and social work.

Whilst the above indicates that that the Guidelines may be very broadly applicable to professionals who are not psychologists, there is then what amounts to a prohibition to the area of gender:

> Statement on the assessment by psychologists of transgender or non-binary people seeking medicines or surgeries associated with gender
>
> Psychologists are reminded that they must practice within their competency (HCPC, 2015; BPS 2017, 2018).
>
> In order to protect the public, the BPS makes clear that in order to assess gender dysphoria or incongruence and make referral for hormonal treatments, anti-androgenic treatments, other medicines; or surgeries such as genital surgeries, chest surgeries, facial surgeries, surgeries which remove reproductive capacity, or other surgeries in this field, psychologists must be statutorily regulated by the HCPC and receive specific post-doctoral training.
>
> This training must be significant formal training and supervision from someone with recognised expertise in the field who has considerable experience in making these referrals. At present this would be a consultant psychologist or consultant medical doctor at an NHS Gender Identity Clinic.
>
> This must occur before they are able to make independent assessments and recommendations. Psychologists in this field must also be practicing within a highly specialist multidisciplinary team and undertaking ongoing specialist CPD relevant to the field.

Initially, after their publication in 2019, the Guidelines would have implied to the reader that they were applicable to the full age range of persons experiencing gender incongruence, as the Guidelines contain sections on both Young People (pp. 12–13) and Older GSRD People (p. 13). However, soon after the publication of the Guidelines, concern was growing about the social transitioning of gender-incongruent children and the use of puberty blockers with minors. Legal challenges were also in train. Following the publication of a letter of concern in *The Psychologist*, the BPS published an online statement as follows:

'we share your concern about the safeguarding of children and young people, but our guidance is specifically for the care and treatment of adults, not children'.[2]

At the time, I considered this to be an insufficient clarification, in a limited location, and this was to form part of my subsequent formal complaint to the BPS. Further reference will be made to this below.

It should be noted at this point that the final paragraph of the BPS statement accompanying the Guidelines is in effect a warning. It carries an implication that there is likely to be something special and different in undertaking work specifically with *Transgender* clients as opposed to *Sexuality and Relationship Diversity*, and that this is the remit of highly specialist experts and services, not just any fully qualified practitioner.

Process of producing the Guidelines of 2019

The Guidelines (British Psychological Society, 2019) state that they are a second edition, hence a revision of a pre-existing document. They are credited to a working party of six applied psychologists and an advisory group of five named individuals. Support was provided by two BPS staff members. The BPS did not consult users/recipients of services when producing the Guidelines. This failure was formally confirmed to me by the Society in response to my complaint (see section below). The BPS chose instead to take advice from two activist organisations, the LGBT Foundation and Stonewall. Furthermore, it appointed as its chair Dr Christina Richards, who was a transgender activist, to manage the process and the meetings.[3] An indication of the position taken by Dr Richards about research on biological transitioning came from their statement in an academic forum: 'sometimes people think there is a debate about that and hopefully I have included enough references for you to think that debate is shut. There is not a debate about this anymore.'[4]

I would argue that, whilst Dr Richards may have *seemed* to be a legitimate choice for the working group, the person appointed chair should have been someone who could mediate controversy, tolerate a lack of consensus, and ensure the representation of the latter in the eventually produced Guidelines. The statement made above by Dr Richards would seem to obviate that. Furthermore, the partisan view of Dr Richards (and of *The Psychologist*—see Chapter 3) is also illustrated within an item published in the latter magazine, around the same time as the Guidelines. This was a featured job: 'Highly Specialised Clinical or Counselling Psychologist'.[5]

> We spoke to Professor Christina Richards, MSc DCPsych CPsychol EuroPsy FBPsS, HCPC Registered Applied Psychologist, Lead Consultant Psychologist & Head of Research, Chair BPS Division of Counselling Psychology, Visiting Professor Regent's University London … 'Consequently, we are looking for people with an interest in the field and an open mind. *The details of Gender Diversity can be learned, but an open and inquiring mind cannot. Bigots and exploitative theoreticians need not apply!* Clever, open people who are interested in clinical practice, research, truly multidisciplinary working, and developing this emerging field are most welcome.' (my emphasis added)

There are accounts supplied to me privately of the process of producing these Guidelines, which suggested a very dominant 'centralised' thrust, and an atmosphere not conducive to respectful and democratic discussion. In light of these accounts to me, at the point of registering a formal complaint to the BPS, I asked this simple question: 'Can all the members of the working party confirm they signed off on the final document?' A direct answer to this question was avoided in all the BPS formal responses, as was any response to how the Society chooses who to appoint to working parties about this or any other policy.

The form and content of the Guidelines

The Guidelines comprise a one-page introduction, eleven pages (some only part page in length) of text under seven headed sections, and one and a half pages of references and 'further reading'. Such complex and controversial areas, which constituted the title and the content of the document, can hardly be adequately addressed in such a brief document. As I will argue below, nuance and elaboration of complexity were clearly never intended by the working group producing the document. Instead, the primary goal was to set out the tenets of an ideology, which the BPS (at the behest of the chair and a selected activist group) is prescribing dogmatically for all practitioners. For comparison purposes, it is worth looking at the more recently published *Working with Autism: Best Practice Guidelines for Psychologists* (2021),[6] which comprises almost forty pages and helpfully addresses contention in the field.

The ideological tenets of the Guidelines are telegraphically conveyed, and are dominated by a concern for the topic of transgender, to the detriment of sexuality. This heavy bias reflects a wider cultural development within identity politics and within organisations such as Stonewall.[7] The latter organisation still drives a pro-trans agenda. This has triggered a split in the organisation, with the formation of the dissenting LGB Alliance. That important schism and the tensions about the concept of transgenderism and its implications for psychological practice were not recognised at consultation, nor were they discussed in the Guidelines. That silence about academic and clinical contestation was a clear indication of the narrow ideology being promulgated.

The silence is particularly relevant to the controversy about 'affirmative' practice in relation to paediatric transition. Critics of the latter point up the tendency of the practice to shepherd anxious and confused gay boys and girls into a reductive biological solution to their existential concerns about their sexuality (not their gender). This pre-empts the option of cautious watchfulness, rather than biological intervention, as the young person matures. The same activist group driving these Guidelines subsequently was to go on to argue that such a cautious approach, rather than being wise, was a new example of 'conversion therapy'. This has been depicted as an extension of the latter practice from the 1960s and 1970s in relation to homosexuality. This claim is being challenged at the time of writing by a range of gender-critical academics and clinicians.

Within the document, a bias towards, and dominance of, gender over sexuality is evident throughout. That imbalance throws into relief the need for a separate consideration of the difficult areas of professional practice in relation to sexuality and relationship diversity. What is left out of the document are ethical and legal implications of professional practice in relation to the latter. These include the common and professionally problematic area of minor attracted persons (MAPS) or 'paedosexuality'. This is not just numerically a common and significant part of 'sexual diversity', but the sexual victimisation of children often emerges from a biographical context of child sexual abuse (CSA). Moreover, that abuse is highly predictive of mental health problems in its survivors both in childhood and later years. This glaring omission of a major policy concern about sexual traumatisation and its consequences is brushed off with the glib 'The guidelines do not, however, relate to anything non-consensual'.

Given the brevity and glaring omissions of the document, the anomalous choice to overly focus on BDSM (pp. 4, 9, and 10) suggests a further example of the ideological bias of the group producing the Guidelines. In particular, the presupposition that diverse identities must at all times be affirmed predominates. 'Identity' has twenty-nine references in eleven pages and is pushed determinedly to prescribed practice. The document is prescriptive and dogmatic. For example:

> Psychologists should integrate an affirmative stance to their models of practice when working with GSRD clients. (p. 7)
>
> Psychologists required to make formal assessment should default to respect for a client's identity or practice. (p. 6)
>
> Robust clinical reasoning should be presented on those occasions when an identity or practice is not supported. In these instances, consideration should be given as to how any GSRD identity or practice could be expeditiously supported in the future. (p. 6)

The moral hazard of what is being prescribed (and proscribed) is not discussed in a spirit of academic caution. Affirmation, as opposed to empathic exploration, too early in the process of assessment is surely unprofessional. However, that risk is not considered but simply ignored in the Guidelines. Many gender-confused young people have not been accorded encouragement and support to engage in listening, talking, and reflection in the hurry for affirmation. Affirmation of a gender identity may be modish for now in transgender therapy culture, but it is also being challenged as poor practice from an opposing clinical and academic position. Only the first stance was asserted in the Guidelines.

The interpersonal, familial, and cultural pressures to 'affirm' (which really means *confirm*) is part of the context of clinical decision making, but the Guidelines offer the reader no reflexive discussion of their own shared cultural context. The professional and client alike in the transaction of affirmation collude in an agreement within that current cultural norm. The client or their family are signalling that, for example, 'Trans women are women. I am trans. I was born in the wrong body and only when I can change my body into a woman will I be okay.' The psychologist in their affirmation of these assumptions is abandoning their duty of care (common in assessments more generally) to explore sensitively what self-statements mean and the options available to do the least harm to the client and improve their mental health.

The conflation of a person/client with identity/ies is a category error. Respect for the *person* who presents to a psychologist is paramount, a *sine qua non* of professional practice. However, 'identity' is a very different category to that of being a person. With that distinction in mind, what does 'Psychologists required to make formal assessments should default to respect a GSRD client's identity or practice' mean?

Respect for a person is not the same as an empathic but questioning approach to their presentation in a clinical assessment setting. An individual person is a fully real entity whose existence has sanctity. An individual's 'identity' develops in childhood and adolescence through greater or lesser psychological turbulences and trauma, and will continue through adult life. Respect belongs with the person. A client will present a snapshot of their 'identity' in the clinic. They will see the psychologist because there are problems (distress and existential confusion).

Even in a few sessions, it often is apparent that 'identity' is complex, unstable, contradictory, and evolving. It may be beset with fear, fantasy, and delusion. Longing for peace, self-acceptance, social approval, and relationship fulfilment may be part of a disturbed sense of self. The client's imagined solutions may be unrealistic, risky, rash, unhealthy, dangerous, and resistant to consideration. This conventional wisdom about cautious exploration, derived from wider clinical practice, is simply torn up and thrown away by the approach encouraged so prescriptively by these Guidelines.

The document indicates that a practitioner's approach should prioritise the role of *social stigma and prejudice* over other factors within formulations of individual distress. 'Stigma' has ten separate references, 'discrimination' seven, and 'marginalisation' six in the less than eleven full pages of the text.

> GSRD identities and practices, just as heterosexuality, cisgender and monogamy, should not be considered to be pathological *although in extremely rare instances* [emphasis mine], behaviours and feelings may be evidence of a mental health condition or acquired brain injury for example. (p. 6)
>
> issues which 'fit' the diagnosis may disappear when the underlying issues associated with being in a group which is subject to prejudice and stigmatisation have been addressed. (p. 12)

I would argue that this pressure to dismiss the incidence of co-occurring mental health or neurological difficulties as 'extremely rare' is highly irresponsible, given the known association of existential confusion and gender non-conformity with autism, family dysfunction, and childhood adversity. No other client group presenting for assessment would be denied an open-minded approach or the full considerations of their life circumstances and personal history in favour of simplistic default to 'affirmation'.

The age ambiguity regarding the pertinence of the document remains within the body of the text. This would appear to relate to the fact that members of the working party were unclear that the Guidelines would later be said to only to apply to adults. The section 6B on pp. 12–13 headed 'Psychologists Should Recognise the Needs and Issues of GSRD Young People and Their Particular Vulnerabilities and Risks' contains the following:

> Psychologists working with GSRD youth should be aware that reproductive options and considerations may be more complex than with their heterosexual or cisgender peers. Assistive reproductive options may be needed and should be discussed openly and frankly, perhaps especially in the case of trans youth who are seeking treatments which will remove reproductive options at an age below that which people commonly consider becoming a parent.

The implication here is that young people who present at clinic, and who wish to receive puberty-blockers and other drug treatments, may be under eighteen, and the implications of these treatments will be discussed. The administration of puberty-blockers to under-eighteens has, since the Guidelines were published, been the subject of legal rulings,[8] medical tribunals,[9] and independent ongoing review.[10] However, none of this important context has led to the BPS issuing amendment alerts to assist practitioners, nor were the recurring cautions in this context rehearsed by the group producing the Guidelines.

I have already suggested that the proviso 'nothing that is non-consensual' betrays a poor grasp of clinical realities. Consensuality is not a binary. It shades into questions of maturing personal consent and, beyond that, into important professional matters of safeguarding for children and vulnerable adults. A practitioner might be well advised, where a vulnerable and distressed person said that they were engaging in masochistic sex, or where a person with a history of being a domestic abuser was engaging in sadistic bondage, to approach the notion of 'it's consensual' with scepticism. What responsible Guidelines would dismiss the relevance of consensuality without so much as a sentence acknowledging its centrality and the difficulties it presents within psychological assessment and practice?

With regard to consent, the NHSEs latest guidance on the legal position (see again endnote 7) states:

> For those aged 16 and 17 (and over 18s) the courts have maintained a position that they are presumed to be able to give legally effective consent to treatment for hormone blockers or cross-sex hormones.

It should be noted that 'legally effective' is not the same as 'psychologically valid' or even, in common-sense terms, 'personally wise', and that the NHSE guidance, in stark contrast to the GSRD Guidelines, acknowledges the limitations of the evidence base that can be used for the 'informed' part of consent: 'For hormone blockers, that includes reflecting on the limited scientific evidence base for their use in this context.'

The GSRD Guidelines are unhelpful in respect to research/evidence base. A useful comparison can be made with the previously cited Autism Guidelines, which are not only far more comprehensive but are preceded by a critical approach and a section on future directions for research. They note helpfully: 'Despite growing interest and research, the evidence base around how best to support people with autism, or which interventions are most effective, needs to be improved' (p. 47). GSRD Guidelines have a mere two pages of selective and sometimes methodologically flawed evidence.

The GSRD chair had already deemed some of the research 'now shut' before the Guidelines were produced. Hilary Cass[11] (appointed by NHS England and NHS Improvement to chair the Independent Review of Gender Identity Services for children and young people in late 2020) indicates in her interim report that the debate is not shut. Her inquiry will address the dearth of basic follow-up data collection and research methodology and commissioning:[12] 'Principles of Evidence-based Service Development' and 'Interim Advice, Research Programme and Next Steps' (pp. 53–76) since 'there are major gaps in the research base underpinning the clinical management of children and young people with gender incongruence and gender dysphoria, including the appropriate approaches to assessment and treatment'.

The tone of the Guidelines

In my view, the GSRD Guidelines were written and published from a flawed process, and their form and content are inherently problematic. This is compounded by, and also reflected in, their tone. Whilst the previously cited BPS Autism Guidelines are informative and discursive, the content of the GSRD Guidelines is expressed throughout in a dogmatic 'Thou shalt' edict form. In the less than eleven full pages that comprise the body of text of the Guidelines, the phrase 'Psychologists should' appears fifteen times in the twenty-seven headings and an additional forty-two times beneath the headings.

Gender incongruence and distress constitute a highly contentious area of psychology, and many now feel anxious to express an opinion in light of that contention. They may be anxious also to engage with clients who, when presenting with family problems, trauma, abuse, or autism, mention gender distress, perhaps alongside possible adolescent social contagion or internet grooming. It is highly unfortunate that practitioners have, in effect, been discouraged from addressing the needs of such clients rather than immediately referring them to GIDS services. The interim Cass report cited previously has indicated that this model of delivery has done a great disservice to such clients.

Given that both the content and tone of the GSRD Guidelines are so unhelpful to practitioners, they surely require a very radical and in-depth review and revision. Without that consideration of the faults discussed above, practitioners will be left without adequate guidance from the BPS. In the absence of such a more considered review, practitioners may be unsure of themselves when encountering vulnerable clients with a label of 'gender dysphoria'. That lack of certainty is amplified by the current Zeitgeist about transgender ideology, within the febrile norms of identity politics.

In the context of work within BPSWatch.com and @psychsoc-watchuk, there have been numerous communications which confirm that these Guidelines have engendered fear, not offered clarity, for practitioners. The following direct quotes of Twitter replies may help to confirm this:

> Thank you for posting this. Our profession is in terrible trouble over this, I feel like (almost) everyone has lost their senses and abandoned their most basic principles. For the record, I wouldn't take on a case like this, purely out of fear for the consequences for me. (Psychologist)
>
> Thank you for this deeply insightful thread! All clinicians are facing these misguided guidelines that put 'kindness' and 'respecting identities' above clinical judgement and what might be best for the patient. (Medical Consultant)

Opposition to the Guidelines

The central concern of this book is the dysfunctionality of the BPS. This has manifested itself in a distinct lack of healthy open debate, let alone dispute or disagreement, about key areas of policy and psychology. It has been argued earlier, with evidence, that a process of active censorship is applied to in-house publications. Members are ignored, individually or collectively, when they raise concerns about the stance or policy adopted by the Society on contentious matters. Formal complaints about this are not properly dealt with.

Censorship and bias have been evident in relation to in-house publications, most notably *The Psychologist*. The general shortcomings of the latter are addressed in my previous chapter and relate to the publication's failed duty to inform members about major occurrences and problems within the BPS as in its stated remit:

> As the official monthly publication of The British Psychological Society, The Psychologist serves as a forum for communication, discussion and debate on a range of psychological topics. We publish a wide range of scientific, professional and personal formats aimed at our large and diverse audience: The Psychologist is read by more than 50,000 Society members in print, and many non-members view our open access offerings online.

In the hard copy, it states differently: 'it provides a forum for communication, discussion and *controversy* among all members of the Society' (my emphasis).

The Psychologist is clearly wary of controversy when and if it threatens the interests of those contingently in charge of the BPS. As disgruntled senior members, some of us formed the blog BPSWatch.com (described in Chapter 3). An account is given there of the active censorship of a paper on sex and gender, where an article agreed for publication was subsequently spiked.[13] The author of the article recounts

> efforts on the part of some to explore the threat of litigation in an effort to constrain serious debate about an important public policy matter and the BPS played its role in this regard. For example, material was deliberately delayed for publication and the editor was instructed to print a letter of complaint sent to the BPS and he was found lacking for not making clear that my view in the original piece was not that of either the Society or the DCP.

Following a High Court ruling of 1 December 2020, that under-sixteens could not give informed consent to taking puberty-blocking medication (since quashed in favour of clinical decision-making),[14] *The Psychologist* immediately published (3 December 2020) a highly contentious article by a trans activist which stated: 'The High Court just dealt a blow to the rights of transgender children in the UK (Bell v. Tavistock, 2020). As a consequence, thousands of trans teenagers have been stripped of the autonomy to access a life-saving medical treatment.'[15]

In the comments section of *The Psychologist*, I challenged this one-sided and unhelpful polemic, which appeared immediately upon the judgement. The publication had clearly failed to consider the predicament faced at this juncture by practitioners. The responses to me by the editor confirmed *The Psychologist*'s bias in favour of the ideology, rather than any properly considered view of the dilemmas now faced by practitioners.

In the previous chapter, I noted that the editor, Jon Sutton, had already commissioned an article by a trans activist, Reubs J. Walsh, and this was sharpened up with editorial help to form an immediate response to the judicial review. Sutton responded to me thus:

> The editorial team approached Reubs Walsh at the beginning of the year, originally about writing (on a voluntary basis) on gender diversity and autism. Inevitably as the legal case developed, that became more of a focus, and as we had the article ready to go (with some amends once the outcome was known), that seemed a good time to put it on the website. Part of a magazine's role is to be topical, particularly with its online presence ... The 'truth' is not always so simple, and the 'law' can be questioned.

The editor also responded to my criticism with this:

> All readers are free to agree with the article (many have), disagree with it, ignore it, as they choose. We will continue to provide that forum for discussion and debate, and will not be stifled by any responsibility to side with a particular position.

However, it is patently clear that the editor has never subsequently approached any actual BPS members or practitioner psychologists to publish any of the debate/discussion on this up to the point of writing. Nor did he cover the centrally relevant Cass report on the subject. A number of members have contacted BPSWatch and told of their letters, which he has failed to publish.

The Psychologist also turned down for publication an article entitled 'Free to think: igniting the fire or filling the vessel?'[16] subsequently published elsewhere in an educational psychology blog (see footnote), which opens with the statement:

> This shift from free speech being regarded as a core liberal value to one where it is viewed as only championed by those with nefarious motivation, has occurred rapidly and has caused consternation, and some conflict, in many institutions and professional groups (e.g. the British Psychological Society).

The Psychologist did publish, but in letter form only: 'Freedom of Expression around Diversity Guidelines: Numerous psychologists call for review of the BPS Guidelines for Psychologists Working with Gender, Sexuality and Relationship Diversity',[17] signed by nineteen senior members, plus four who wished to remain anonymous due to career anxieties.

Whilst there were detailed comments in response, which continued the discussion, letters which appear with comments online only are less likely to be seen and read. By contrast, those placed in the hard copy of the magazine are read routinely by BPS members. A bland 'Society Response' followed the letter, and no attempt to acknowledge and address the concern of these senior practitioners was forthcoming.

In this context, BPSWatch has been contacted by members who have tried to engage in ongoing communications about their concerns with BPS officers and staff. Elected officers usually fail to engage and hand the concern to staff. Senior staff have implied that polite, relevant persistence is bullying and cited the Code of Conduct back at individual members. In other words, contra the claims about welcoming a discussion of controversy, both the editor of *The Psychologist* and his employers utilise a range of tactics to suppress debate and silence unwelcome dissent from ordinary members.

My complaint

Historically, the BPS reputation for the way in which it has dealt with complaints, including adhering to its own published procedure, is notoriously poor. Along with other concerned members, the view of the Charity Commission was expressed in their reply to me, dated 4 November 2020, which stated:

> We are currently engaging with the society over a number of issues and have found deficiencies in some areas of operation. Whilst I would expect the charity to have a robust and well managed complaints process, this may have not been the case in the past.

I had made a very detailed complaint about the Guidelines and about a key player in the production of the Guidelines. The complaint was made in August 2020 and closed in April 2021. Most of the substance of the complaint was not upheld, although an external investigator did give some support to some points that I had made.

The BPS failed to follow its published procedures of the time in several ways, for which there was an apology. They did agree as a matter of urgency to make explicitly clear on the Guidelines that they relate to over-eighteens only (but, as indicated above, the text remains ambiguous). There was some acknowledgement that a future revision might consider whether the remit was too wide in including sexualities, this having been suggested by the investigator.

The details and outcomes of my complaint are marked by the BPS 'Strictly Private and Confidential', but despite requests for clarification, I am not clear which parts are covered by this and which are not. One example is the matter of my detailed critique of the bias and unreflective approach to research and the evidence base. The BPS response was not only wrong, it was shocking for a supposed learned society. I would like to expand on this, but to cite the response from the BPS verbatim would risk disciplinary action against me. Suffice it to say that in response to my statement within my complaint that 'The data on outcomes is limited, inconclusive and fraught with methodological issues, and there is in the community of mental health professionals globally a debate and a view that further research is needed', the BPS did not agree.

The gist of their response was that there was a strong international medical consensus among professionals who specialise in transgender healthcare regarding standards of care. The response failed to note, though, that such a temporary consensus is driven by transgender activists and is currently receiving substantial opposition from gender-critical professionals. Again, we find this failure on the part of the BPS to note controversy and debate despite its rhetoric to the contrary. They brushed aside any controversy in the mainstream with a lack of considered exploration—'there will always be some dissenting voices'. They were categorical in their response that any idea that there was any real schism in the scientific community was false. Following the lead of Dr Richards, the firm view of the BPS was that the evidence base was just fine.

Why the debate is far from 'shut'

As noted above, the BPS's chosen chair of the group producing the Guidelines has expressed the view, very publicly, that the 'debate is shut' concerning the biomedical transition of young people and adults. In *The Psychologist* 'Featured Job' referenced in footnote 5, it was made very clear again by Dr Richards that any contrary view reflects 'bigotry' (see Chapter 3). The brevity of the Guidelines is also a reflection of a 'debate is over' position.

The professional literature, when properly reviewed (which was not the case in relation to these Guidelines), indicates that the debate has only just begun. This unresolved contestation has three main aspects. First, for now there is no empirical evidence that the prescription of puberty-blockers, cross-sex hormones, and surgeries leads to mental health gain for identified patients (Dhejne et al., 2011). Second, there is clear evidence that those interventions (introduced into bodies which are perfectly healthy) lead to significant medical risks (Butler & Hutchinson, 2020; Cohen & Barnes, 2019). Third, there are serious ongoing ethical arguments that children in this clinical group are unable to give informed *and valid* consent to what are clearly life-changing biomedical interventions.

The informed consent challenge in relation to this clinical group has two key aspects: the lack of clear information to transmit to patients and their families, and the immature cognitive capacity of children. On the first count, to be informed, any decision requires valid information. As was noted above, that evidence base for now remains missing. On the second count, children are recognised usually as being limited in their capacity. They cannot buy cigarettes or fireworks. They cannot get married or consent to sex. They cannot obtain a tattoo or a piercing.

Despite these norms outside of the clinic, affirmative practices in service norms are encouraging children to agree to long-lasting changes to their body. Their lack of appreciation of sexual satisfaction or any future need for parenthood is ignored in favour of practices which are *de facto* forms of castration and the removal of reproductive rights, all of which bring with them iatrogenic risks. The wide-ranging literature that has considered these matters was simply ignored by those producing the Guidelines. If that silence in the Guidelines is in any doubt, the reader can consult (amongst others): Brunskell-Evans and Moore (2018), Levine (2018), Marchiano (2017), Olson (2016), Pilgrim and Entwistle (2020), Saad et al. (2019), Steensma et al. (2017), and Stagg and Vincent (2019).

These ethical and empirical concerns were not represented *at all* in the Guidelines. In wider disputes about transgender rights on social media, such concerns are typically dismissed by activists as being transphobic or 'anti-trans'. Such a dismissal reflects a persistent and dogmatic 'the debate is shut' line of reasoning. If that dismissal is in doubt, anyone even wanting to debate the matter is described as a 'bigot' (see my previous chapter).

A supposedly research-based, learned, and professional society such as the BPS should have eschewed the premature certainties being claimed by trans activists. It failed quite spectacularly in this respect. Admittedly, the BPS is far from isolated in this regard; the results of activist capture are evident across a number of professional bodies globally today. The most significant of these has been the guidelines of WPATH (World Professional Association for Transgender Health), which have been generated by trans activists and their allies from academia and clinicians working in specialist transitioning services. These have proved an invaluable back-up source of supposed legitimacy, when cited by activists seeking to reduce continuing open and reflective debate.

What had started as a service in the Netherlands in the 1990s as a *pilot model* has been seen to expand incautiously in Europe and

North America into a *service norm* (de Vries & Cohen-Kettenis, 2012). When some clinicians expressed the need to pull back from this evidence-free service expansion, and instead exercise cautious watchfulness, they were criticised, their employment terminated, and their services to young people closed down, under trans activist pressure.

This was the fate of the Canadian clinical psychologist Ken Zucker (Zucker, 2012). In Britain, the psychiatrist David Bell was disciplined for raising his ethical and empirical concerns about the Gender Identity Development Service at the Tavistock Clinic. This has created an anxious concern in mental health workers. For example, a very senior clinical psychologist messaged me privately recently, saying, 'I wouldn't touch gender issues with a barge pole—instantly refer on and ignore the fact that the client will suffer. I would avoid it like the plague.'

However, despite these current anxious concerns in practitioners, the interim report from Hilary Cass in England, cited above, may mark a significant turning point. She has now formally registered a clear caution about the poor evidence for clinical efficacy available and the risks this now creates for patients. Her review has confirmed the reasonableness of the criticisms and cautions proposed by those like Zucker and Bell. She also draws attention to the biased priorities created by the creation of specialist services in this field. Those biases have emerged systemically because specialist services are the sites of ideological capture by activists.

Distortions in healthcare service developments also arise from commercial interests: drug companies and career-orientated clinical specialists. These shaping pressures in services are now very well documented (Alford, 1975; Biggs, 2018; Dhalen, 2020; Hilário, 2019; Ioannidis, 2018; Williams et al., 2011). In light of that evidence, far from the debate being 'shut', the future of transgender healthcare remains highly contested (Pilgrim, 2021).

Final reflections

I have argued that the Guidelines in form, content, and tone are in themselves evidence of ideological capture within a dysfunctional organisation. The BPS itself exists in a social context, in which identity politics are for now normative (albeit controversial). Also, members have noted in recent times within the BPS a proliferation of newly titled, highly paid posts and, in such a climate, the continuing attraction of new business income streams becomes paramount. It is no surprise that lack of accountability in the organisation would give free rein to opportunism. In fact, it would enable a non-psychologist CEO to feel able to attend crucial government departmental policy meetings solo without being encumbered by complex and unfashionable caveats, which any accompanying psychology practitioners might bring up.

For any reader who is inclined to see the writer as a conspiracy theorist, in respect of the claimed permeation of trans activism, I would refer them to the advice given by the law firm Dentons, in particular this article:[18]

> Dentons' report states that every child has an accurate conception of their own gender identity which they should be entitled to affirm in law without impediment. 'The right to legal gender recognition is crucial for young trans persons to secure all other rights', it states, advising that the UK should 'eliminate the minimum age requirement' at which children can change their legal gender 'on their own volition, without the need for medical diagnoses or court determination'. The Dentons document emphasises that there should be 'no eligibility criteria', such as medical or psychological interventions. And UK authorities should 'take action' against parents 'who are obstructing the free development of a young trans person's identity in refusing to give parental authorization when required'.

I have elsewhere argued that the Guidelines represent a serious failure, not only for professional psychologists but also their clients and the general public.[19] Nowhere more so than with these Guidelines do we need to pause and consider what first principles should apply:

> Statement of values: Psychologists value their responsibilities to persons and peoples, to the general public, and to the profession and science of Psychology, including the avoidance of harm and

the prevention of misuse or abuse of their contribution to society. (BPS Code of Ethics and Conduct, 2018)

The singular expression of one version of identity politics, in this case transgender activism, is neither a democratic nor research-based guide for good professional practice. Such a dubious adherence to dogma is clearly at odds with the rhetorical ethical aspiration just cited from the BPS. My arguments above have sought to elaborate this point of conclusion.

Postscript

Since this chapter was finalised, it has been announced that the Tavistock GIDS single specialist provider has been deemed 'unsafe' and is to be closed.[20] A new, more integrated service for gender-questioning children is to be provided from regional centres. The spin that was put on this announcement by those supporting the trans activist stance, Stonewall, Mermaids, and also by the British Psychological Society, was that the primary driver for this was unacceptably slow access due to lengthy waiting lists. In fact, it had been confirmed that the service operated a predominantly 'affirmative, non-exploratory approach, often driven by child and parent expectations' and that there was 'limited evidence of ... a discipline of formal diagnostic or psychological formulation'. Children and adolescents should 'receive the same standards of clinical care, assessment, and treatment as every other child or young person accessing health services'.[21]

The BPS has prevaricated in committing to reviewing its 2019 GSRD Guidelines variously depending on the outcome of the Bell vs. Tavistock judicial review, following the outcome of the appeal against that review, and then on Twitter 'following the Cass Review'. Accordingly, I wrote to the BPS on 16 August 2022 noting how ambiguous this position had been, given that the existing Guidelines were supposedly 'for adults only'. I asked for clarification of the following:

- Are the GSRD Guidelines being reviewed?
- Would a review result in guidelines for children and young people?

- Should revised Guidelines separate gender from sexuality and relationship diversity?
- Has the BPS reflected upon better process and outcome for reviewing the Guidelines?

I stressed the duty of the British Psychological Society in this regard:

> In recent service delivery for gender questioning and distressed children and young people, the foremost service, GIDS, has been *psychologist-led*. It is therefore astonishing that there have been no effective guidelines for psychology practitioners forthcoming from the BPS as our professional body. The BPS must grasp this situation and take a lead.

No answers have yet been forthcoming.

Notes

1. www.bps.org.uk/news-and-policy/guidelines-psychologists-working-gender-sexuality-and-relationship-diversity; or https://web.archive.org/web/20220108004620/https:/www.bps.org.uk/sites/www.bps.org.uk/files/Policy/Policy%20-%20Files/Guidelines%20for%20psychologists%20working%20with%20gender,%20sexuality%20and%20relationship%20diversity.pdf (in case the 2019 Guidelines themselves are made unavailable for future reference).
2. https://thepsychologist.bps.org.uk/volume-33/october-2020/freedom-expression-around-diversity-guidelines
3. http://christinarichards.co.uk
4. www.youtube.com/watch?v=usyYi3Cevdo (@ 40 minutes 30 seconds in)
5. https://thepsychologist.bps.org.uk/volume-32/june-2019/featured-job-highly-specialist-clinical-or-counselling-psychologist
6. www.bps.org.uk/news-and-policy/new-best-practice-guidelines-working-autistic-people
7. www.stonewall.org.uk/about-us/blog/trans-equality-heart-stonewall%E2%80%99s-mission-%E2%80%93-and-won%E2%80%99t-change
8. www.england.nhs.uk/commissioning/spec-services/npc-crg/gender-dysphoria-clinical-programme/update-following-recent-court-rulings-on-hormone-blockers

9. www.bbc.co.uk/news/uk-wales-61213539
10. https://cass.independent-review.uk
11. Dr Hilary Cass, a former president of the Royal College of Paediatrics and Child Health, was appointed by NHS England and NHS Improvement to chair the Independent Review of Gender Identity Services for children and young people in late 2020.
12. https://cass.independent-review.uk/wp-content/uploads/2022/03/Cass-Review-Interim-Report-Final-Web-Accessible.pdf
13. https://bpswatch.com/2021/02/07/david-pilgrims-disappearing-article
14. https://en.wikipedia.org/wiki/Bell_v_Tavistock#High_Court_judgment
15. https://thepsychologist.bps.org.uk/blow-rights-transgender-children
16. https://edpsy.org.uk/features/2021/free-to-think-igniting-the-fire-or-filling-the-vessel
17. https://thepsychologist.bps.org.uk/volume-33/october-2020/freedom-expression-around-diversity-guidelines
18. www.rollonfriday.com/news-content/dentons-campaigns-kids-switch-gender-without-parental-approval. Note that quite quickly this pro bono advice from Dentons to LGBT campaigners was withdrawn from its website: www.lawgazette.co.uk/obiter/dentons-goes-bashful-over-transgender-children-campaign/5102607.article
19. https://bpswatch.com/2021/09/19/the-british-psychological-society-failing-the-public
20. https://cass.independent-review.uk/wp-content/uploads/2022/07/Cass-Review-Letter-to-NHSE_19-July-2022.pdf
21. www.bmj.com/content/378/bmj.o1916.full

References

Alford, R. R. (1975). *Health Care Politics, Ideological and Interest Group Barriers to Reform*. Chicago: Chicago University Press.

Biggs, M. (2018). The Open Society Foundations and the transgender movement. *4th Wave Now*, 18 May.

British Psychological Society (2019). *Guidelines for Psychologists Working with Gender, Sexuality and Relationship Diversity*. Leicester: British Psychological Society.

Brunskell-Evans, H., & Moore, M. (Eds.) (2018). *Transgender Children and Young People: Born in Your Own Body*. Newcastle: Cambridge Scholars Publishing.

Butler, C., & Hutchinson, A. (2020). Debate: The pressing need for research and services for gender desisters/detransitioners. *Child and Adolescent Mental Health, 25*: 45–47.

Cohen, D., & Barnes, H. (2019). Gender dysphoria in children: Puberty blockers study draws further criticism. *BMJ, 366*: l.5647.

Dahlen, S. (2020). De-sexing the medical record? An examination of sex versus gender identity in the General Medical Council's trans healthcare ethical advice. *The New Bioethics.* https://doi.org/10.1080/20502877.2020.1720429

de Vries, A., & Cohen-Kettenis, P. (2012). Clinical management of gender dysphoria in children and adolescents: The Dutch approach. *Journal of Homosexuality, 59*(3): 301–320.

Dhejne, C., Lichtenstein, P., Boman, M., Johansson, A. L. V., Långström, N., & Landén, M. (2011). Long-term follow-up of transsexual persons undergoing sex reassignment surgery: Cohort study in Sweden. *PloS One, 6*(2): e16885.

Hilário, A. P. (2019). (Re)Making gender in the clinical context: A look at how ideologies shape the medical construction of gender dysphoria in Portugal. *Social Theory and Health, 17*: 463–480.

Ioannidis, J. P. (2018). Professional societies should abstain from authorship of guidelines and disease definition statements. *Circulation: Cardiovascular Quality and Outcomes, 11*(10): p.e004889.

Levine, S. B. (2018). Informed consent for transgendered patients. *Journal of Sex and Marital Therapy, 45*(3): 1–12.

Marchiano, L. (2017). Outbreak: On transgender teens and psychic epidemics. *Psychological Perspectives, 60*(3): 345–366.

Olson, K. R. (2016). Prepubescent transgender children: What we do and do not know. *Journal of the American Academy of Child and Adolescent Psychiatry, 55*: 155.e3–156.e3.

Pilgrim, D. (2021). Transgender debates and healthcare: A critical realist account. *Health,* October. https://doi.org/10.1177/13634593211046840

Pilgrim, D., & Entwistle, K. (2020). GnRHa ('Puberty Blockers') and cross sex hormones for children and adolescents: Informed consent, personhood and freedom of expression. *The New Bioethics, 26*(3): 224–237.

Saad, T. C., Blackshaw, B. P., & Rodger, D. J. (2019). Hormone replacement therapy: Informed consent without assessment. *Journal of Medical Ethics, 105*: 611.

Stagg, S. D., & Vincent, J. (2019). Autistic traits in individuals self-defining as transgender or non-binary. *European Psychiatry, 61*: 17–22.

Steensma, T. D., Wensing-Kruger, A., & Klink, D. T. (2017). How should physicians help gender-transitioning adolescents consider potential iatrogenic harms of hormone therapy? *American Medical Association Journal of Ethics*, *19*(8): 762–770.

Williams, S. J., Martin, P., & Gabe, J. (2011). The pharmaceuticalisation of society? A framework for analysis. *Sociology of Health and Illness*, *33*(5): 710–725.

Zucker, K. J., Wood, H., Singh, D., & Bradley, S. (2012). A developmental, biopsychosocial model for the treatment of children with Gender Identity Disorder. *Journal of Homosexuality*, *59*(3): 369–397.

CHAPTER 5

Policy capture at the BPS (2): the memory and law controversy

Ashley Conway

In recent years, there has been a greatly increased awareness of the widespread scale and significant adverse consequences of child sexual abuse (CSA). The British False Memory Society (BFMS) is a registered charity which promotes the idea that large numbers of adults report CSA as a result of 'false memories'. This chapter examines how the BFMS has attained policy capture in the BPS over the past twenty-five years, to the detriment of victims of abuse. Failures of good governance are identified as a relevant cause of this process.

For much of the twentieth century, the existence of CSA was barely acknowledged, by either mental health professionals or society in general. Since the 1980s, a number of notable celebrities have publicly discussed their own stories of abuse and their personal consequences (e.g., Oprah Winfrey, Roseanne Barr, Sinead O'Connor). More and more ordinary people began to speak up about their own experiences of CSA. The world gradually began to realise that the sexual abuse of children was widespread.

Epidemiological evidence linking adverse childhood experience to the increased probability of adult mental health problems became substantial and incontrovertible.[1] As survivors of CSA have higher risks for multiple mental health problems, including increased risk of self-harm and suicide, fit-for-purpose guidance from the BPS may literally be a matter of life and death.

In the USA, historically, child sex abusers had been protected by statutes of limitation, meaning that a report of abuse had to be made within a certain period of time of the offence taking place (e.g., seven years) for the claim to be considered for prosecution. As a consequence of this time constriction on reporting, when the children became adults, and understood the personal and societal significance of the crime that had been committed against them, it was often too late to seek justice. A statute of limitations is, of course, designed to protect the defendant, and in the case of CSA, it is likely to disadvantage the victim. The law began to catch up, and time bars were greatly extended or abandoned. While child abusers had once believed that after many years they were safe from prosecution, now that comfort was fast fading.

The false memory syndrome (FMS) theory was born in the USA. Apart from individuals wanting to avoid conviction, there was a whole other, wider group of people who just did not want to believe that claims of CSA being widespread could possibly be true. Many in society could not bear the reality of what was unfolding. This laid the terrain for a comfortable explanation for the epidemic proportions of the reports of abuse: they were a consequence of therapists putting those beliefs onto the heads of their vulnerable clients. The therapists were creating 'false memories' of abuse. And if the psychologically vulnerable people had not seen a therapist, then their imagination could be fired by reading certain books related to abuse.[2] The argument went that 'FMS victims' were not lying but were being brainwashed by ill-informed therapists on a witch-hunt, who believed that CSA was everywhere and had to be dug out in therapeutic sessions. The client would come up with a story of abuse, and subsequently mistakenly believe that was an accurate and true memory of what had happened to them, and this was the explanation for all their woes. So goes the FMS line.

The American False Memory Syndrome Foundation (FMSF) was formed in 1992. Both the US and UK activist originators came from family contexts in which CSA had been claimed. It is illuminating to be aware of the roots of the organisations (i.e., the backstories of the founders). The man credited with having coined the term 'false memory syndrome' was Dr Ralph Underwagger. He was one of the co-founders of the FMSF, along with his wife, Hollida Wakefield, and Pamela and Peter Freyd, in March 1992 in Philadelphia.

In 1993, an article in *Paedika*, a Dutch paedophile magazine, reported Underwagger as saying that paedophilia could be seen as a responsible choice and that having sex with children could be seen as part of God's will.[3] The other co-founders of the FMSF, Pamela and Peter Freyd, had been accused privately by an adult daughter of abusing her in childhood. In 1995, Peter Freyd's brother, William, wrote 'the False memory Syndrome Foundation is a fraud designed to deny a reality that Peter and Pam have spent most of their lives trying to escape …'.

In the UK, the BFMS was set up by Roger Scotford in 1993, becoming a registered charity in 1994. He was accused by two daughters of abusing them.[4] The BFMS also set up a scientific advisory board of impressive experts. One of those was Karl Sabbagh, who was convicted in 2019 of grooming a child for sex and only removed from the BFMS Scientific Advisory Board after his conviction was reported nationally in the media in 2021.[5]

Note that these FMS groups are *not* learned societies. They are *campaigning* organisations with an agenda. They have a particular line that they are pushing, and they are very good at it. Both the US and UK groups created an excellent 'communications' strategy, promoting a partisan line of FMS to both the academic community and the popular press. The FMS organisations depicted themselves as the true scientists, while the therapists allegedly inducing these false memories were a bunch of quacks. Appropriate demands of confidentiality meant that therapists were unable to cite the experiential evidence of the abused clients with whom they were working.

To understand the FMS line, we need to take a look, not just at what is said, but also what is *not* said. To start with, what is said, there are three pillars of FMS theory: there is no such thing as traumatic amnesia; FMS is triggered by therapy; and laboratory studies tell us about repeated abuse. I now take these in turn.

1. There is no such thing as traumatic amnesia.
    The BFMS Advisory Board membership is dominated by academics,[6] who will inevitably have different experiences to clinicians. Part of

the BFMS line is that if someone has been traumatised by abuse, then they would always remember it: 'Sexual abuse is easy to remember and extremely difficult to forget. Genuine victims unfortunately cannot repress or forget what has happened to them.'[7] Therefore, somebody apparently 'remembering' abuse is having a 'false memory', and their account should not be taken seriously.

2. FMS is triggered by therapy.

The BFMS website refers to something they call 'recovered memory therapy',[8] which they say

> is renowned for implanting false memories. Following *intensive therapy*, patients are exposed to and become vulnerable to suggestion. For example, a therapist may ask a patient to imagine what it would be like to be raped. After imagining what it would be like, some patients later believe that they were raped. Practitioners of recovered memory therapy believe that buried in the psyche of every adult are detailed memories of every experience from birth. Therapy is administered to unlock these supposedly repressed memories. False memories can also be created through the use of guided and imaginative imagery, and through therapeutic suggestion and hypnosis. (emphasis added)

3. Laboratory studies tell us about memory of repeated abuse. The FMS groups promote the idea that laboratory studies (usually with students) of inducing false memories of relatively trivial events[9] inform us about memory of repeated abuse in childhood by a supposed caregiver.

How valid are the FMS claims?

Having outlined these three core assumptions of FMS advocates, I now address their validity. The BFMS claims about always remembering trauma may seem credible from a common-sense point of view, particularly to those with no knowledge of trauma. However, what is thought of as common sense does not always correspond well to scientifically validated experiences of people who have been repeatedly abused from a young age. The science shows us that people who have been traumatised can, and do, have episodes of amnesia for all or parts of a significantly traumatic experiences.[10] There is robust scientific evidence that when children experience *more* extreme abuse, and from a family member, it is actually *less* likely to be recalled.[11] Ross Cheit has provided us with his own story of recovered memory[12] and has collected an extensive archive of cases where accuracy of delayed recall has been proven.[13]

The idea that reports of abuse are 'dug out' in therapy sessions is in stark contrast to the experience of clinicians (therapists) working day in and day out, hearing stories of abuse, frequently with a fractured timeline and gaps in memories. The science supports the clinicians' experience—and disproves these unscientific claims of the BFMS. Moreover, evidence derived from scientific studies of consequences of CSA is that recall is most frequently triggered *outside* of the therapeutic setting, and has nothing at all to do with therapists.[14] Ironically, on its own website, the BFMS[15] provides us with some actual data on the type of therapy used by individuals allegedly having false memories: of 129 of their cases available, they tell us that only *one* had 'regression therapy'. In other words, their own facts are a far cry from the story they promote.

FMS advocates have a problem with conducting laboratory research to support their case. For obvious reasons, it is ethically impossible to try to experimentally induce a false memory of repeated abuse by a close family member. The notion that artificial laboratory studies to induce relatively trivial memories of single events has any equivalence to people recalling repeated experiences of CSA has no scientific basis whatsoever.

The FMS's stated position is that it is not about deliberate lying, but about genuine mistakes in memory, so it is worth examining the scenarios under which mistakes might emerge. When there is an accusation, there are four possible ways of understanding this: two kinds of true and two kinds of false. Memories may be 'positive', that is believing that something did happen, or 'negative', believing that something did not happen. For example, a false positive would be 'I was abused by person X' (when in fact they were not); a false negative would be 'I have never been abused' (when in fact they have been). If we accept the notion of false memories, both positive and negative are important.

The BFMS tell us about false positives—that an individual can have a false memory of being abused implanted by another person. One of their difficulties with 'claiming the science' is that it is extraordinarily difficult to prove that someone has not been abused—and therefore it becomes virtually impossible to prove scientifically that an accusation is completely false. What they do *not* tell us about is false negatives, that is, a person can believe that they were not abused when they were.

As noted above, there is abundant scientific evidence that traumatic events can be lost from recall, and the science tells us that false negatives can and demonstrably do occur. Yet the FMS want to promote the unprovable idea of the first as the real science, while denying the scientific reality of the latter. The FMS groups use all of their communications and PR skills to promote this biased reporting of the science to professional colleagues and the media. What they do not want to talk about, that is, the science that they deny, is extremely important. Their unilateral focus greatly helps the accused, and greatly disadvantages the alleged victim.

An explanatory critique of the FMS claims

So why would anyone take the FMS line seriously? Firstly, their explanation is simple. 'I'm being accused because someone has filled my daughter's head with nonsense.' This is much easier to understand than the delayed reporting of being abused over a long period of time by a family member. Second, it makes a great headline—'Innocent man sent to prison' is a much more grabbing title than 'Guilty man convicted'. Third, as a society, this belief enables us to continue with a more comfortable (though untrue) notion that the scale of child abuse is being exaggerated and is really a trivial matter. The BFMS do not say what people do not want to hear, but they do say what many already believe and want to persist in believing.

Given the above biased ideology, with its selective attention about the science from the FMS, as well as the widespread cultural complicity of many in the population in trivialising the scale of CSA, what stance has the BPS taken? The answer is that it has colluded actively with that ideology and has contributed to a culture of complicity about the scale and consequences of CSA.

FMS/BPS entanglement and policy capture

The BPS did well at their first attempt (in 1995[16]) at producing what was widely considered to be a balanced and fair report, but then reversed this achievement in a document produced in 2008, slightly revised in 2010.[17]

Two subsequent attempts by the BPS, in 2013 and 2018, to produce guidance documents (which looked like they were going to be much more balanced) were abandoned.

The 2008 report was produced by the BPS Memory and the Law Committee chaired by Professor Martin Conway (no relation to the author here). Note that in 2011 he became a scientific advisor to the BFMS. Professor Dan Wright was another member of the 2008 committee, who is today listed as a scientific advisor to the BFMS. Similarly, Professor Elizabeth Loftus, who was a scientific advisor to the American FMSF, is listed as an advisor to the 2008 BPS committee.

In the 2008 report, there is a striking absence of accurate, in-depth consideration of dissociation in response to traumatic events, and the consequent effects on selective amnesia and recall. This is important, because it is these documented consequences of trauma, including CSA, that provide an understanding of the false negative experience of not recalling a trauma that did occur. This omission is very much in line with the selectively lopsided campaigning focus of the BFMS.

A selective emphasis on the false positive in the BPS report is further evident in its discussion of the prospect of professional therapeutic manipulation: 'It is noted that the impact of therapy on trauma memory has been a concern in the arena of the "false memory debate" for recovered memories of childhood sexual abuse.'[18]

The 2008 BPS report is aligned neatly with the BFMS campaigning position, which focuses on supporting those claiming to be falsely accused of sexual offending, while failing abuse victims who may have experienced a period of amnesia, or have other reasons for delaying reporting their abuse.[19] Reasons for this failure of balance by the BPS may include having influential voices in multiple roles, in contravention of good governance and Charity Commission guidelines; more on this bias created by conflicts of interest now.

Controversy within the BPS about the convergence

The chair of the 2008 committee, Professor Martin Conway, was at that time with the University of Leeds. Of the ten other academics on that committee, four were from the same institution as the chair, who appears also to have been their head of department. In addition to these two roles, at the time of the establishment of the committee, Professor Conway was also chair of the Research Board and a trustee of the BPS.

So, given this particular constitution of a BPS committee considering the topic of memory and the law, how were they chosen? We do not know, but it is noteworthy that five of ten were from the same institution and that no proper governance scrutiny from the BPS dealt with this scenario of potential bias.

The committee produced a document which the BFMS would have been pleased with. There was no acknowledgement of false negatives, and almost nothing on traumatic amnesia. In 2011, the BPS committee chair went on to formally become an advisor to the BFMS.

Through 2012, the British media were running regular stories on the prolific, recently deceased serial paedophile Jimmy Savile. Despite this, between May 2013 and April 2014, there were numerous articles in *The Psychologist* (the house journal of the BPS) sympathetic to the false positive story favoured by the BFMS. In that period of time, the magazine contained no balancing stories related to dissociative amnesia in victims of abuse producing false negatives. When challenged about this imbalance by this author,[20] the editor[21] replied: 'Neither *The Psychologist* nor The British Psychological Society has links with the British False Memory Society.'

This flat denial is at complete odds with the fact that the chair of the BPS Memory and the Law Committee became a member of the Advisory Board of the BFMS, and at that time world-famous FMS advocate Elizabeth Loftus was on the International Panel of associate editors of *The Psychologist*.

While the BFMS Advisory Board has an explicit common goal of supporting the policy stance of the BFMS, the outdated 2008 BPS guidance is unrepresentative of the wider range of positions adopted by its membership. Surely, voices beyond the narrow Leeds-based group, with its *a priori* selective focus on false positive decision-making, should have been included, but they were not. Was the policy capture maintained by the unclear and distorted BPS processes of selecting a chair, and a group of like-minded people, some with multiple roles in the Society? And was this directly related to poor governance?

In 2013, there was an attempt to produce a more balanced report, but this was swiftly shut down by the BPS *with no explanation*. In 2018, there was a second attempt to produce an updated and more balanced document. This group was concerned to alert their own discipline to the social epidemiology of CSA and its sequelae. Their rationale draws upon a wider literature including recent inquiries and official reports, which confirm that CSA has been widespread, and has been met with a complicit response from many in society.[22] An exploratory scoping meeting was attended by representatives of the 2008 report and its new critics.

From this meeting, it was agreed that a new review group should be set up to consider all relevant views. This new committee was re-branded as the 'Memory Based Evidence', or MBE, group. Such a review would shift from the narrow and restrictive framing of memory by BPS members aligned with the political stance of the BFMS to one which now also considered the evidence on underreported sexual abuse and its proven impact on adult mental health. Sadly, such a sensible re-appraisal was *blocked yet again* by the BPS. In 2020, it was shut down in an announcement by Professor Daryl O'Connor, who had been one of the Leeds group of authors on the 2008 report, and by then was chair of the BPS Research Board, and also a member of the Board of Trustees of the BPS.

This was an example of a trend, noted in other chapters of this book, of an influential individual in dual or multiple roles. It was ill-judged that someone who was a member of the 2008 committee would appear to be allowed any influence over the closure of the committee that would replace it. The explanation offered for the termination was primarily a 'lack of consensus' within the group, reframing the very reason that the review was *set up* in 2018 as a reason for its *closure*. The explanation was therefore preposterous.

The BPS threw the revisionist group a bone: they could take the discussion to a journal by writing articles for a special issue of *Legal and Criminological Psychology*. It is unfortunate, to say the least, that the chosen journal has on its editorial board two or three individuals with very close ties to the BFMS. Conflicts of interest seem to abound as a result of poor governance in the BPS, and here was another example.

Professor O'Connor had four relevant roles: he was a named contributor to the 2008 report, he was chair of the Research Board that set up the 2018 group, he was chair when it was terminated, and he was on the Board of Trustees. All of this is in direct contravention of Charity Commission guidelines that trustees should avoid dual roles. As with so many things to do with the BPS, the systems of who chooses the groups and who chairs is, to say the least, opaque.

A great snapshot of the problems in governance and transparency from the BPS is visible in the chain of comments online in response to the closure of the 2018 group.[23] There are twelve comments there from ten contributors (two wrote twice). Eight of the ten are clinical/ applied psychologists and two are academics, who were both chairs of the Research Board, both were trustees of the BPS, and both were named authors on the 2008 report, one as chair, and the other was chair of the Research Board when the 2018 project was terminated.

The chair of the Research Board that terminated the 2018 group states:

> Unfortunately, the standards of evidence for the report and the need for consensus … could not be met … A meeting of the members involved … was held in January 2021. This was a constructive and helpful meeting, and the former members of the … group agreed a way forward: rather than reconstitute the group they will first work on a series of articles about memory-based evidence for a special issue of a relevant journal.

Those from the group of eight applied psychologists were universally critical of the BPS's actions in closing the project down. Here is a selection of comments from these critics:

> I am, of course, aware that the subject is contentious but it is quite baffling that the group could not even produce a report acknowledging this …

Referring to court cases where witnesses, memories of events are disputed:

> a psychologist asked in court what their professional body's view on such memories would be 'It doesn't have one.'

Questioning the BPS line that contributors could write for a special edition of a journal:

> Is a 'series of articles' equivalent to an official position statement? Will they ever be written? Does this help a psychologist acting as a witness in matters of memory? My answers? No, probably not, and no.

The next contributor was a member of the BPS Research Board, which was responsible for the closure of the MBE group. Referring to the correspondent above, he states that he 'rightly asks':

> Does this help a psychologist acting as a witness in matters of memory? .... Unfortunately, in the light of inadequate BPS Guidelines some psychologists and psychiatrists acting as Court Appointed Experts routinely dismiss reports of Child Sexual Abuse. These are matters of life and death!

Elsewhere,[24] referring to the structuring of the 2018 MBE group, the same author states:

> I started to feel uneasy when a person was appointed as chair who seemingly lacked clinical practice experience and for a decade had worked in a public sector organisation strongly associated with a 'Discourse of Disbelief'. It dawned on me that the Terms of Reference were inadequate (as I feared when I first saw them). Before the October 2020 Research Board meeting a recommendation was made by two senior BPS officials (who had been members of the group developing the controversial 2008/2010 document) to close the ... group as in their view its frame of reference objectives could not be met. I was surprised by the level of apathy and disinterest at the BPS Research Board. It is my view that the BPS, like many such organisations worldwide, has failed to adequately inform its members, other professionals, and the public about the nature of sexual abuse trauma and its consequences. The British Psychological Society has a

duty to inform its stakeholders about the realities of extreme abuse and its consequences that show up in mental health issues.

The next comment is from a member of the terminated 2018 group:

I am unhappy about the Research Board's decision to disband the group, and I do not think that there has been a satisfactory answer to why such a decision was made; this decision was made without consultation with the group members, nor with the wider Society ... The Group's work had not progressed to any review stage as this statement suggests, but it is my belief that the work was not far from completion. I am confident that the Group had high standards for the presentation of evidence, as well as honestly presenting the gaps in what is known ... It was also clear that the document should clearly lay out contemporary understandings of how trauma impacts upon memory. I am very concerned that our learned Society is not leading on this area, especially in light of the various national and international inquiries which are taking place on trauma. I think the Society's silence here leaves a worrying vacuum ... I am not alone in feeling unhappy about the Society's behaviour towards the work of Group and there are others who are dissatisfied with the 'alternative solution' to take aspects of the work forward. I would ask the BPS to reconsider its decision, and to explain why this is the second time that it has stopped this important work proceeding.

The next comment notes:

Having worked in specialist NHS trauma services for 24 years, I have assessed and treated hundreds of clients who have suffered abuse and torture. Their memories of this trauma have varied from 'photographic' to vague. I have treated many clients who have become aware of abuse years later, often when something else happens to trigger the memories. Without ... up-to-date guidance, outdated tropes about False Memory Syndrome will prevail. What has happened here? Why aren't we being told what has happened in a clear and straightforward way? The BPS works for its members and for the general public … The British False Memory Society had a man (convicted as a sex offender in 2019) sitting on its scientific and professional advisory board for over 20 years. This is not a coincidence. Those who seek to undermine the credibility of genuine survivors will not stop publishing their thoughts and attempting to influence guidance. Well-informed, expert evidence is the only way to challenge this. The BPS must find a way to produce guidance on this matter. A series of articles will be completely useless … It is simply not acceptable or responsible to duck the issue because it is hard.

I added my comment:

The 2008 report implies that academics conducting lab research, with students about memory of relatively trivial incidents in childhood, makes them the experts on matters of trauma and delayed reporting of abuse. By not updating the Guidance, the BPS colludes with this folly, to the detriment of its reputation as a serious scientific body. This collusion is nothing short of shameful, and apart from being a breach of its obligations under our Royal Charter, Statutes, and Charity Commission regulations, it is a gross institutional betrayal of its members, and more importantly fails to prevent the re-victimisation of some of the most vulnerable members of our society.

Another clinical psychologist writes:

From Jimmy Savile, Rotherham and Oxford child sexual exploitation scandals, the abuse in children's homes, sporting and religious organisations through to Weinstein, sex trafficking and #MeToo, the past ten years have exposed the extent of abuse in our society. The current Independent Inquiry into Child Sexual Abuse (IICSA) has heard evidence from 5,104 victims and counting. Given this, and the massive impacts on people's lives, don't we have a duty to present the state of the evidence as accurately and clearly as possible, acknowledging the limits in our knowledge, and areas where the evidence is in dispute …?

The evidence base is significantly stronger and clearer than it was in 2008 … Failure to produce clear and definitive guidance on this issue fails victims, defendants, those who work with them (including BPS members) and the public.

The chair of the BPS 2008 report and FMS advisor, Professor Martin Conway, added his comments, referring to an inaugural meeting of those interested in joining the 2018 group:

Unfortunately, I found it unfocussed and fractionated and decided to leave after an hour or so … As I left the room my last bit of advice to them was 'Stick to the science' … It should have been easy for a small group of well-informed researchers to have updated the original report and its advice … Perhaps if they had taken up my offer from over 10 years ago we would now be in a much better place.

With this 'take it or leave it' approach from Martin Conway, and his persistence with a selective view of what the science said, there was no sign that newer critics would have their voices heard. By closing down the group, which by its very existence was meant to take a fresh look at *all* the evidence relevant to its topic, by default this older view continued to prevail on record as the policy stance of the BPS. Accordingly, by default, the BPS was supporting the campaigning claims of the BFMS, with the chair of the 2008 report as the influential bridge between the organisations.

Reflections on the policy capture

So there we have it, in 2021, the chair of the BPS 2008 group and FMS advisor telling us that we should 'stick to the science'. But surely good science is not selective, favouring one group or another, while failing to address evidence in its totality? The suggestion that the update should have been easily carried out by non-clinical researchers continues the exclusion of practice-based evidence, and lacks any clarity of what, exactly, 'research' means. And perhaps we should have taken his advice over ten years ago? In many ways, these comments appear to be representative of the BPS position, and reflect a lack of insight into what is needed for the genuinely scientific exploration of this field.

There are only two voices in this chain that broadly support the actions of the BPS on shutting down two attempts to produce unbiased scientific guidelines. They have both been chairs of the Research Board, both been trustees, and both authors of the outdated 2008 report (one as chair), which needs to be replaced.

Whatever the reality of the effects of the two individuals having double or triple roles, it is very definitely not a 'good look'. It is not just that in the BPS a minority have very significant power, but this minority are completely out of touch with the thoughts and needs of their applied colleagues. It is a clear example where failures of governance, procedures, and transparency by the BPS have created a problem, which in this case may result in some of the most vulnerable members of our society being put at greater risk of harm.

Who are the current (2008) guidelines benefitting? The answer to that depends on one's focus. Clinicians and victims of abuse are not being supported. As for expert witnesses and lawyers, the answer is ambiguous. The 2008 policy position from the BPS favours those working for the defence but not the prosecution. It certainly favours the FMS campaign, and the problems of bias that this overlap of roles and networks can facilitate are demonstrated above.

How do campaigning groups get away with claiming the science, while giving us a one-sided story? Why do the media and even alleged science publications still continue to fall for this (e.g., the BBC[25] and *New Scientist*[26])? Answering that question brings us back to the wider cultural complicity in society about the denial of the scale of CSA. We don't want to know that our uncle, neighbour, youth group worker, favourite celebrity, and so on, has a sexual interest in children. It's uncomfortable. But to create change, we have to look squarely at the reality and the evidence. As a professional society, the BPS should be confronting that denial and promoting courage in facing up to the reality. So far, the BPS has failed to do that.

The Society needs to increase understanding amongst clinicians, academics, the media, and the general public of the effects of trauma on memory. This is the most ethical way to best serve those who are already disbelieved, or have the reality of their memories called into question by the misuse of data derived from experimental psychology.

With intelligent, unbiased policy statements and guidance, the BPS could help inform expert witnesses and lawyers, who would otherwise be using disinformation in a way that is misleading to juries. With academics, researchers, clinicians, expert witnesses, and the media fully informed, understanding in society at large will follow.

There needs to be appropriate transparent governance to ensure inclusion in committees producing policy documents. These committees should include a diversity of specialist opinions and research methodologies. Clinicians, researchers, and other experts in CSA, trauma, and dissociation should have a clear voice. This proposal for open and representative discussions in the BPS challenges its norms to date of poor governance more generally.

Many questions need answering. Who is deciding what a BPS policy is on anything? This is a very simple question, but it seems impossible to get clear answers from the BPS. Good governance needs to start with the Board of Trustees, which is in complete disarray at the time of writing. For now, the Society shows no sign of serious intent to address the dual/multiple roles of some members of the Board of Trustees.

Poor governance has enabled, and will continue to enable, cabals and policy capture. Policy capture can harm people. The BPS needs to be consciously and visibly separate from the influence of pressure groups. There needs to be transparency about group selection, visible inclusivity, and fit-for-purpose committees and chair selection. Chairs should adopt a position of equipoise and be open-minded about the views of their colleagues. Members of policy committees should not be trustees. The above account of the capture of the topic of this chapter by the 'Leeds group', with its FMS allegiances personified by the committee chair Martin Conway, demonstrates that the BPS cannot ensure representative and reflective forms of policy development. All the expectations of good practice I have just listed have been ignored by leaders in the BPS.

With some irony, the chair of the 2008 committee, Martin Conway (who, as we will remember, had also been a chair of the Research Board, a member of the Board of Trustees, and an advisor to the BFMS), when referring to the first meeting of the doomed 2018 group, said this: 'Who appointed the members of this group, I have no idea …'.

It is tempting to believe that all the failings detailed in this chapter are down to incompetence. At the beginning of 2022, the BPS initiated yet another new group to create guidelines in this field. In April 2022, both the editor of this book and myself received copy-and-paste notifications that we would not be invited onto this committee because 'your expertise was not specifically related to memory, which is the topic of this work'. Both of us have published relevant books on the topic,[27] and this author received a major international award for his edited book on trauma and memory.[28]

Since then, I have been asking the Society who *has* been selected for that group. They will not provide me with that information. After many years of bias in the output of the BPS on this topic, I have come to the conclusion that the problem is not simply a matter of incompetence. I now believe that the BPS does not have the will to produce a document which is genuinely balanced and helpful to victims of childhood trauma.

Notes

1. A. Saied-Tessier (2014). *Estimating the Costs of Child Sexual Abuse in the UK.* London: NSPCC; *Improving the Response to Child Sex Abuse in England.* London: UK Children's Commissioner's Office.
2. E. Bass, & L. Davis (1988). *The Courage to Heal.* New York: Harper & Row.
3. M. Orr (1998). False memory syndrome movements: The origins and the promoters. In: V. Sinason (Ed.), *Memory in Dispute.* London: Karnac.
4. Ibid.
5. S. Delahunty (2021). www.thirdsector.co.uk/charity-reports-itself-regulator-third-sector-alerts-sex-offender-advisory-panel/governance/article/1706388.
6. https://bfms.org.uk/advisory-board
7. https://bfms.org.uk/what-is-false-memory
8. Ibid.
9. E. Loftus, & J. Pickrell (1995). The formation of false memories. *Psychiatric Annals, 25*: 720–725.
10. American Psychiatric Association (APA) (2013). *Diagnostic and Statistical Manual of Mental Disorders* (5th Edition). Washington, DC: APA; and WHO (1993). *The ICD-10 Classification of Mental and Behavioural Disorders Diagnostic Criteria for Research.* World Health Organization, Geneva.

11. L. M. Williams (1994). Recall of childhood trauma: A prospective study of women's memories of child sexual abuse. *Journal of Consulting and Clinical Psychology*, *62*: 1167–1176.

12. A. Conway (2022). In conversation with Ross Cheit. In: *Trauma and Memory: The Silence and the Silenced*. London: Routledge.

13. https://blogs.brown.edu/recoveredmemory/case-archive

14. J. Goodman-Delahunty, M. A. Nolan, & E. L. van Gijn-Grosvenor (2017). *Empirical Guidance on the Effects of Child Sexual Abuse on Memory and Complainants' Evidence*. Sydney, Australia: Royal Commission into Institutional Responses to Child Sexual Abuse; P. A. Stavropoulos, & C. A. Kezelman (2018). *The Truth of Memory and The Memory of Truth: Different Types of Memory and the Significance for Trauma*. NSW, Australia: Blue Knot Foundation.

15. https://bfms.org.uk/bfms-archival-study. When is the issue of false memory raised in historical child sexual abuse allegations? An archival study of 496 British cases. J. Shaw, M. Leonte, G. Ball, & K. Felstead. Table 2.

16. J. Morton, B. Andrews, D. Bekerian, C. Brewin, G. Davies, & P. Mollon (1995). *Recovered Memories: The Report of the Working Party of the British Psychological Society*. Leicester: British Psychological Society.

17. British Psychological Society (2008/2010). *Guidelines on Memory and the Law: Recommendations from the Scientific Study of Human Memory*. Leicester: British Psychological Society.

18. Ibid.

19. A. Conway, & D. Pilgrim (2022). The policy alignment of the British False Memory Society and the British Psychological Society. *Journal of Trauma and Dissociation*. https://doi.org/10.1080/15299732.2022.2028222

20. A. Conway (2014). BPS—Obsessed with the False Memory Syndrome? *The Psychologist*, *27*: 302–303.

21. J. Sutton (2014). Memory matters. *The Psychologist*, *27*: 303.

22. Goodman-Delahunty et al., *Empirical Guidance on the Effects of Child Sexual Abuse on Memory and Complainants Evidence*; D. Pilgrim (2018). *Child Sexual Abuse: Moral Panic or State of Denial?* London: Routledge.

23. https://thepsychologist.bps.org.uk/volume-34/april-2021/not-good-look# comment-406

24. https://psychassessmentblog.wordpress.com/2021/10/25/bps-memory-based-evidence-task-finish-group-a-matter-of-life-and-death

25. www.bbc.co.uk/programmes/m00114br; https://dissociativecooking.wordpress.com/2021/11/08/104

26. www.newscientist.com/article/mg25133551-000-repressed-memories-the-dangerous-idea-we-cant-seem-to-forget

27. D. Pilgrim, *Child Sexual Abuse*.

28. V. Sinason, & A. Conway (Eds.) (2022). *Trauma and Memory: The Science and the Silenced*. London: Routledge.

CHAPTER 6

An organisation without a memory?

David Pilgrim

A glaring irony mentioned on a few occasions in this book is that we have a psychological society that has proved itself to be psychologically incompetent. One specific aspect of this has been the apparent failure of those leading the organisation to learn from experience.[1] For now, the BPS is neither a convincing learned body nor a credible learning organisation.

My historical sketch to defend that claim has two overlapping parts. The first describes the legacy, from the end of the nineteenth century, of naïve realism and how this has limited critical self-reflection within the discipline of psychology. The second examines how that limitation has been amplified by recent managerialism in the BPS, with its anti-intellectual and anti-democratic tendencies.

Problems old: the failures of naïve realism

During the first half of the twentieth century, before Karl Popper challenged the naivety of positivism with his critical rationalism,[2] British psychologists pursued the aspirations of Ward and Rivers that I cited in Chapter 1. Naïve realism was to be expressed in two main forms in the psychology departments being established in the academy in the mid-twentieth century.

The first was that of *experimentalism* of the 'Oxbridge model' of psychological science. This began with psychophysics and the eventual preoccupation those in this laboratory tradition had with 'controlling out' the messiness of the fluxing open system of human life in the real world.[3] The second was *statistical*, in particular focusing upon the use of psychometrics to make factual claims about differences between and within populations. This tradition was developed predominantly in the Psychology Department of University College London (UCL).

Though these were methodologically different approaches, they both reflected the dominance of two philosophical bedfellows: empiricism and positivism. The first of these limited knowledge claims to consensual agreements about what observers witnessed with their senses. The second extended this and considered that science incrementally described lawful relationships, verified by empirical evidence or justified by tautological reasoning ('covering laws').[4] Reality was deemed to be positively present and repeatedly verifiable, empirically, by scientists in all contexts (the assumption of 'empirical invariance', across time and space). Empiricism was driven strongly by the legacy of British philosophy, whereas its bedfellow of positivism was developed more in France, becoming influential elsewhere (including Britain).[5]

These naïve realist assumptions, though strongly held, were flawed for a number of reasons, pointed up by Karl Popper. His views were extended and debated by Jürgen Habermas in the 1960s, especially in relation to the value-saturated social sciences.[6] The debate was to continue within the philosophy of science, raising several doubts about positivism, which included the following.[7] Science cannot be disinterested because it is a social activity, and so scientists will always, knowingly or not, reflect the value system of their own cultural context. Moreover, the empirical detachment being claimed, with some confidence, by natural scientists is questionable in psychology, because we are both subject and object: the test tube looks and talks back at the human scientist.[8]

Also, reality is not only positively present (the limited purview and reach of positivism), it is also absent. Real mechanisms exist in the world, which are not seen and are not always activated,[9] but they are real. Positivism offers us only a very thin surface account of reality ('ontological monovalence'). Most of reality is absent from us, and so critical, rather than naïve, realism works with this new assumption of absence as well as presence. With that absence comes mystery and complexity: what do we know for certain about anything, when it comes to ourselves and our relationships with others? There is a further challenge facing naïve realism in psychology: it relies on consistent personal integrity. This is a cue for the next sub-section.

How the mighty have fallen

If scientific results are obscured from scrutiny, or they are fabricated, then Popper's aspiration for self-regulation in the scientific community is stress-tested to breaking point. Some psychologists (and other scientists) have been charged with deceit, data fabrication, and selective interpretations in order to support an ideological position. Some have failed to sustain their claims because others have been unable to replicate their findings (within the experimentalist wing of positivist psychology).

For reasons of space, I will prioritise the first of these problems (i.e., versions of alleged cheating), with our focus on British psychology.[10] In the case of the 'replication crisis', this has emerged beyond the boundaries of both Britain and psychology as a discipline. Both of the examples I now offer about charges of fraud emerged in the statistical tradition of eugenic reasoning, seeded by the Victorian patriarch of British eugenics, Francis Galton. He set up the first Chair in Eugenics in 1911 at UCL. Its occupant was the mathematician Karl Pearson, who was both a racist and a socialist.

The contradictions Pearson embodied were not unusual at the turn of the twentieth century. At that time, many liberals and social democrats were eugenicists. Indeed, until the Nazis later were to give eugenics a very bad name, the aspirations for human improvement, via socially engineered genetic policies, were common across the political spectrum.[11] For example, some first-wave feminists promoting birth control, like Marie Stopes, were evangelical eugenicists. Another wider consideration, for the reader new to the topic, is that British eugenics was more about class than race. However, later arguments in and about the UCL tradition of psychology were to implicate both.[12]

The baton of the eugenic tradition was carried from Francis Galton to Karl Pearson to Charles Spearman to Cyril Burt to Hans Eysenck. Between them, Pearson and Spearman developed much of the conceptual infrastructure of modern-day behavioural statistics taught to undergraduates (including factor analysis, correlation, the Chi square test, and probability distributions).

Leaving aside the debate about judging past knowledge claims by the standards of current identity politics,[13] we can note the mainstream acceptability of eugenics as part of the *social context of emergence* of the work of Cyril Burt and Hans Eysenck. Their presence in British psychology was enormous in the twentieth century, so doubts about their integrity, even weighed up posthumously, have implications for the present credibility of the discipline.

Uniquely, Burt was president of the BPS for two consecutive years (1941–1943). His role in shaping the system of secondary education after the Second World War is now recognised, and he was a pre-eminent leader in educational psychology.[14] Burt succeeded Spearman as Professor of Psychology at University College in 1932. He had affirmed the Spearman–Pearson position on 'innate general cognitive ability', which could be 'objectively determined and measured'.[15] After the Second World War, Burt's advice to policy-makers continued in his Eugenics Society lecture on 'Intelligence and Fertility'. His posthumous papers restated his presuppositions about genetic determination of cognitive capacity, which remained unchanged throughout his life.[16]

After his death in 1971, Burt was accused of falsifying his data in some studies and even inventing the existence of his co-workers providing the data. Lesley Hearnshaw, in his sympathetic, but ultimately critical, biography, noted:

> Burt had a good cause to defend, but he made two major mistakes. He used doubtful means in the defence of his position: and in *defining* intelligence as 'innate cognitive ability' he in effect begged the question. He should have restricted his definition to 'general cognitive ability', leaving the issue of its innateness and its degree to be determined empirically. Had he done this he would have avoided a good deal of trouble and criticism. (emphasis in the original)[17]

A small literature has debated what Hearnshaw called 'posthumous controversies'.[18] As I have noted elsewhere, the 'Burt scandal' is a distraction from a central feature of biogenetic studies. The eugenic axiom about hereditability *preceded* empirical evidence; the latter played only a selective confirmatory role.[19] This is the pointed insight offered by Hearnshaw about Burt 'begging the question'.[20]

Burt may or may not have made up data (and people) to confirm his eugenic ideology. In my view, he was guilty, but my judgement or any other here is not germane. Either way, what is important is that eugenicists were tempted to massage their data and interpret it in certain ways to sustain a biogenetic *assumption*. This point also then applied to one of Burt's PhD students.

Uses and abuses of psychology[21]

If Burt was the dominant patriarch of British psychology by the middle of the twentieth century, that mantle was arguably taken over by his student Hans Eysenck. He was an émigré who, along with others, arrived to revitalise the de-theorised naïve realism of the British empiricist tradition I noted earlier and in Chapter 1.

Eysenck was a high-profile controversialist, spending much time on public displays and communication about psychology. He tended to leave the spade work of research and its applications to his clinical colleagues, such as another émigré, Monte Shapiro. For example, he purportedly led the behaviour therapy movement in Britain. However, he saw very few patients to defend his authority in practice.[22] His public rhetoric emphasised, like Ward and Rivers, cited in Chapter 1, fearless fact-finding:

> I always felt that a scientist owes the world only one thing, and that is the truth as he [sic] sees it. If the truth contradicts deeply held beliefs, that is too bad. Tact and diplomacy are fine in international relations, in politics, perhaps even in business; in science only one thing matters, and that is the facts.
>
> (Eysenck, 1990, p. 229)[23]

In light of his masculinist public bombast as a truth-seeker, today it is ironical that Eysenck's questionable provocations about the presumed role of psychological genetics in the understanding of cancer might well be his posthumous undoing. He was funded by the tobacco industry to pursue a line of research to problematise the link between smoking and lung cancer. Conveniently, he developed a model entailing a cancer-prone personality, and when this intersected with addictive behaviour (also genetically loaded) then lung cancer was raised in probability.

The commercial value of this model to the tobacco industry is obvious. If lung cancer was driven by the psychological make-up of the smoker, then this diverted attention from the political, moral, and financial liability of the tobacco industry. It is an alternative narrative to the traditional critique of the tobacco companies seeking to addict the population with a carcinogenic product for profit. Favourable research then might augment tobacco industry advertising.

In 2019, King's College London[24] investigated Eysenck's work about this topic, which had been co-authored by Ronald Grossarth-Maticek. The investigation was instigated by a complaint from Anthony Pelosi[25] about the studies. It concluded that indeed their findings were 'unsafe' and incompatible with expectations of good clinical research. Pelosi himself had already described the work as 'one of the worst scientific scandals of all time'. He drew attention to a wide range of published critiques of the research from a range of journals. Pelosi had tried and failed in 1995 to prompt the Institute of Psychiatry and the BPS to review the evidence. He was shut down quickly by both organisations. Eysenck was still alive, which may have inflected the anxieties of those in power. Posthumous reviews risk no challenges about libel.

The conclusion then from King's was suitably and appropriately damning, even if the exercise had taken over twenty years in the making, with the BPS still dragging its heels. In a re-run of the problems of Burt's data, the inquiry agreed with the published critics that the findings were statistically implausible. In the wake of the King's College investigation, most of the journals informed of the findings retracted the work of Eysenck and Grossarth-Maticek (prompting the latter to threaten legal proceedings). So far, eight journals have retracted a total of twenty articles. Four journals have looked through their archives and attached expressions of concern to a total of sixty-five authored and co-authored papers by Eysenck on topics other than fatal diseases. One of these is from as far back as 1946.

The matter then of Eysenck's credibility as a disciplinary leader in British psychology has many loose ends. The judgement about him is a work in progress. If King's College had started their critical look back, then how might the BPS address this unfinished business? This is a cue for the next section.

Problems new: the failures of managerialism

After his death in 1997, the BPS established an annual memorial lecture in Eysenck's name. It can be put alongside the annual award of the Spearman Medal[26] as an indication that the biogenetic legacy, started with Pearson in the Galton Chair of Eugenics in 1911, was seen by the Society as prestigious and honourable, rather than dubious or shameful. Pelosi, in his critique of Eysenck and Grossarth-Maticek, cited papers critical of their work published since the 1990s. Despite this available public literature, casting doubt upon the cancer research, posthumous accounts of Eysenck continued to be hagiographic.[27]

For example, in 2016, Philip Corr provided a lengthy celebration of his work in *The Psychologist*.[28] This mentions his work on cancer but reports it uncritically. Corr does note, though, that Eysenck was not in favour in Britain compared to the USA; for example, he was never awarded a fellowship by the BPS. Eysenck's reputation as an outsider, who was never embraced and properly respected by British psychology in the academy, is a trope repeated in his autobiography and by his hagiographers.[29]

Pelosi, and others such as David Marks,[30] lobbied the BPS to follow up the King's College investigation, and indeed in 2021 the Ethics Committee set up a look-back exercise on Eysenck and the prestigious Galtonian tradition in British psychology and the Society. Marks wrote to the CEO of the BPS, Sarb Bajwa, in December 2018 requesting an urgent review of Eysenck's work. This letter received no reply.

On hearing of Bajwa's return after his year's suspension, in November 2021, Marks sent a prompting letter reminding him of his failure to answer the 2018 letter; note there had been *three years* of radio silence.

However, this time a response was forthcoming, not from Bajwa, but from one of those he managed. He passed it down to Rachel Scudamore ('Head of Quality Assurance and Standards'), who replied to Marks:

> We accept that a failure to respond is discourteous and that it would leave you in a position of not knowing what action has been taken. I can only apologise on behalf of the Society for this error on our part. (Marks, personal communication)

The delay and the manner in which it was then dealt with are consistent with points raised in other chapters about poor responsiveness to members from the centre of the BPS. Scudamore's use of the first-person plural indicates a shift from the moral responsibility of the CEO to the diffuse corporate responsibility of the organisation. 'We' can be everybody and nobody.

By this stage, it transpired that the BPS had indeed instigated a review of Eysenck's work but had not broadcast that fact (see above). Had Marks not pressed more, we are left to speculate whether the BPS membership would have ever known this fact.

The Burt scandal re-run but in a new context

I noted earlier, *pace* Hearnshaw, that Burt's work 'begged the question' derived from ingrained eugenic thought within twentieth-century British psychology. In my view, the same point can be made about the 'Eysenck scandal'. As with his mentor, Hans Eysenck crassly took for granted: (1) that psychological characteristics were overwhelmingly genetically determined; and (2) that the term 'inherited' referred to such a chromosomal legacy. The presumptuousness of the first point passed with little or no reflection about its origins in society, particularly in relation to the political movement of eugenics.

The presumptuousness of the second point was queried by one of his lesser recognised (note: female) contemporaries, Alice Heim, when discussing the problematic concept of intelligence.[31] She noted that, by the 1950s, it was well proven that intra-uterine health shaped child development. Thus 'inherited' (if we mean 'born with') refers to congenital impacts as well, and so it has an *environmental* component. As with Burt and the other eugenicists in the Galtonian tradition, Eysenck was not really going to let the facts (despite their sacralised status from Ward and Rivers onwards and his own rhetoric) get in the way of his ideology. Heim later confronted Eysenck with the limitations of his eugenic reasoning in relation to race and intelligence, and he offered his dismissive reply.[32]

Eysenck's funding from the tobacco companies (which, note, he solicited) certainly casts doubts on the model he conveniently developed.[33] However, of equal importance was that Eysenck operated biogenetic assumptions more generally in his work, not just in relation to this topic of cancer. Now these considerations are being judged not just in the academy but also in the managed world of the BPS.

For reasons explained in previous chapters, we have few grounds, for now, to trust the intellectual integrity of those running the Society; its status as a learned body is in substantial doubt. In light of the explorations begun earlier in the book about how the new managers (since 2018) have been operating, the faltering exchange between Marks and managers in the BPS warrants reflection.

Bajwa did not respond in 2018 at all. However, this was not unusual during that period. And then there is the interesting devolution of accountability. Why did a subordinate (Scudamore) reply and not Bajwa himself? After all, he must have *received* the letter from Marks, in order to pass it 'down'. Why did he not just apologise? Was it 'beneath him' to do so? Might it have required a credible *explanation* for his rudeness or oversight?

I do not know the answers to these questions, but they would not need to be posed, at the time of writing, had Bajwa taken action on receiving the letter in the first place in 2018. He could have seen the warning signs being offered by concerned critics like Pelosi and Marks. He could have acted promptly *and transparently* to ensure the BPS itself now reviewed the matter properly. Maybe he did act promptly but, if he did, then neither Marks nor the BPS membership were apprised. A pattern was becoming evident of an inward-looking leadership culture with secretive and mendacious tendencies. The word that might best connote that trend is 'cabal'.

The function of organisational amnesia for the cabal

The word 'cabal' informally has been used often by critics writing in this book, as an alternative to more neutral terms like 'leadership'. Its negative connotation reflects a value-judgement, born of the experience of ordinary BPS members encountering obfuscation. It intimates a sense of toxic leadership, described by Graham Buchanan in Chapter 2.

However, whatever the words used, the struggle to describe what has been happening at the centre of the BPS, since the turn of this century, is not merely a semantic matter. 'Something is rotten in the state of Denmark'[34] (or, in this case, Leicester). Another ancient adage invited is that 'a fish rots from the head down'. As writers in this book all confirm, *something* was happening that was, to say the least, dark and suspicious. This misgovernance necessitated forms of deceit and wilful blindness from those defending the organisational status quo.

By 2000, the shaping of the Society by the new public management (NPM) model was in full swing, and its first CEO was appointed then. He left under a cloud and no clear historical record exists of why, though rumours abound. By 2018, the NPM approach was in overdrive. The new managers (with authoritative business titles of 'Directors'[35]) joined the new CEO to flex their muscles in the BoT. They attended as employees and not full members.[36]

However, the extent to which this mattered as a democratic concern needs to be put in the context of most of the psychologists on the BoT being *appointed* internally. This happened with few clear rules, other than invitation and networking, or because they were chairs of other Boards in the Society (and so with their own agenda and interests to pursue). The presidential triumvirate was certainly there as a sop to democracy. However, its version referred to the membership, not outsiders in the civil society, who were supposedly being served by the charity.

The treatment of recent presidents suggested that the culture at the centre was not going to afford them an easy ride, if they expected to change much. Being a titular and biddable president ensured a quiet life and an enhanced CV. Being a turbulent one risked scorn and disparagement. The centre was politically fraught, and there was no hiding place for radical critics. The chances of honest historical reflection were slim in this cultural landscape. It was probably like trying to meditate while being bombed in the middle of a war zone.

A sketch is not enough and the paradox of managerial rhetoric

I have taken the liberty above of offering a broad sketch of a toxic leadership culture, where an emergent cabal was inheriting and reshaping the norms and mores of the old oligarchy. However, it is possible that for reasons to be determined with time, I am simply wrong. What is problematic about my description is that it is *necessarily* sketchy.

The reason for this is that new forms of managerial rhetoric have intensified in recent years to cover up the operations of an inner sanctum of power. This is the 'bullshit' I will explore further in Chapter 7. Obfuscation has been the overarching tendency in the leadership culture ('cabal' or otherwise). This process of incessant mystification is the recent backdrop to how the BPS is likely, for now, to deal with the thorny question of its own history, *especially that in living memory*.

Having made these general points about the threat of new forms of managerialism to historical candour, there is a paradox. The new managerial rhetoric, amongst other things, emphasises organisational learning from adverse events, with the particular notion of a 'learning organisation'. If the NPM model was to operate according to its own criteria of best practice, to deliver a genuine learning organisation, then it would *enhance*, not obstruct, a proper historical account. One way we can demonstrate this point is to apply an immanent critique.[37]

The latter is an approach to claims about reality, which discerns whether they are consistent with their own expectations. In this case, rather than a critic directly expressing their anger or disappointment about how the BPS is being run, or about a particular topic of interest to them, instead they can step back and check on the *premises of probity espoused by the managers themselves*.

In this case, I will utilise in this chapter and the next the aspirations listed in the *Strategic Plan 2015–2020*. This covered the period when the NPM was already established but was now to operate with clearly stated aspirations for efficiency and probity. This was the very period when the SMT was installed, the CEO was suspended, a major fraud took place in the BPS, and the membership were so disaffected that many left and some of those staying were provoked into angry campaigning. Here are the criteria from the *Strategic Plan*:

- rigour and fairness;
- honesty and integrity;
- transparency;
- respect for a diversity of viewpoints;
- the highest standards of professionalism and ethical behaviour, atti-tudes, and judgements, as laid out in our Code of Ethics and Conduct.

So, to apply an immanent critique to the above item by item, with an eye to the ease with which we could piece together a clear history of the BPS during the period specified, we can say this:

1. The policy capture in the BPS described in Chapters 4 and 5 demon-strates that processes in the BPS are neither fair nor rigorous.
2. The whole of Chapter 7 is an analysis of why the management culture of the BPS *lacks honesty and integrity*. The structural flaw present since 1965 of a board of faux trustees, with their inevitable conflicts of interest, has compounded this problem.
3. Whatever else we can say about events in recent years, there has *not been transparency*. In Chapter 3, Pat Harvey explains why the normal and reasonable expectations of public knowledge about the BPS as a charity broke down. Wilfully, or by unconscious default, the functioning of the Society was being obscured from public view. In reaction, this encouraged and necessitated the development of a blog and Twitter account to reveal what the managers of the Society wanted to keep under wraps. In response, those managers closed down the Twitter account (twice) and threatened the new bloggers with legal action to desist from discussing a material fact (that the CEO was suspended in November 2020). Silence in *The Psychologist* about the crisis confirmed this deliberate management policy of politically driven obfuscation.
4. There has been a managerial defence of a *highly biased and non-inclusive approach to diversity of views*. Again, the earlier chapters in policy capture demonstrate this point. We have many examples of both individual and multi-signed letters of concern about policy matters being wilfully ignored.
5. The final criterion is important because it demonstrates that those who have tried to operate with integrity about probity in the Society,

such as presidents MacLennan, Kinderman, and Hacker Hughes, have been scorned and resisted. *The notion of 'professional standards' has been manipulated* by the BPS leadership to close down legitimate criticism and to exclude needed corrective action about misgovernance.

The above immanent critique reveals that the recent management culture of the BPS has failed miserably, according to the criteria it claims to set for itself about probity. The BPS is not formally a public body, compared to clearer-cut cases like the NHS. However, it is a charity and its claims about its research base as a discipline, and its applications in its professional wings (represented by the Divisions) should at all times act in the public interest. This intention should be seen to be done. If this does not happen, then why would the BPS have a charitable status at all, and why should the public trust its research claims, practitioners, and policy advisors?

Conclusion

Any historian, investigative journalist, or forensic accountant would be challenged to piece together a clear and coherent recent history of the BPS and the events it has contained. In the first part of the chapter, I explained the generic problems in the discipline (and often wider) about research integrity. By those older criteria of academic hygiene, discerning the past misdemeanours of those like Burt and Eysenck was going to be faltering and its utility open to debate. However, it was at least possible in principle, according to Popperian aspirations for self-correction in science. If we were left with that older frame of reference alone, to provide honesty and integrity, it would not be straightforward, but efforts could be made to succeed.

That struggle for clarity in the academy has been complicated now, though, by the failures of modern managers (in the case of the BPS and other dysfunctional organisations) to live up to their own rhetorical expectations about transparency. In the second part of the chapter, I applied an immanent critique to demonstrate this point and the material in all of the chapters in this book would seem to be confirmatory. The reader can make their own judgement.

Notes

1. The need to learn from experience requires an organisational memory to work and be sustained on an ongoing basis. This was the point of the paper issued by the Chief Medical Officer for England in 2002: L. Donaldson (2002). An organisation with a memory. *Clinical Medicine*, 2(5): 524–527.

2. Popper argued that the opportunity for falsification (refutation) is important in scientific activity rather than verification (proof). He had confidence that science could be self-correcting with its ensured free expression and constant efforts between competing researchers to confirm or disconfirm the work of others.

3. This is about the study of correlations between dependent and independent variables in the closed system of the laboratory, rendering any extrapolation of findings to the open system of everyday human life problematic (see Chapter 1).

4. G. C. Hempel (1942). The function of general law in history. *The Journal of Philosophy, 39*: 35–48.

5. The British empiricist tradition was articulated by David Hume, John Locke, and George Berkeley. The roots of positivism were to be found in France (the work of Comte, St Simon, and Laplace). By the twentieth century, they were melded in much of psychology in the Anglo-American academy, until its disruption by the postmodern turn (see Chapter 1).

6. K. Popper (1959). *The Logic of Scientific Discovery*. London: Routledge; J. Habermas (1972). *Knowledge and Human Interests*. London: Polity Press.

7. A more elaborate account can be found in D. Pilgrim (2020). *Critical Realism for Psychologists*. London: Routledge.

8. D. Bannister (1966). Psychology as an exercise in paradox. *Bulletin of the British Psychological Society, 19*: 21–26.

9. R. Bhaskar (2016). *Enlightened Common Sense: The Philosophy of Critical Realism*. London: Routledge.

10. A longer version of material in this section is available in D. Pilgrim (2022). Verdicts on Hans Eysenck and the fluxing context of British psychology. *History of the Human Sciences* (in press). https://doi.org/10.1177/09526951221143888

11. By the middle of the twentieth century, social psychiatrists such as Aubrey Lewis, who was the first Medical Director of the Institute of Psychiatry in London (and managed Eysenck there), were eugenicists. My own liberal professor (Lesley Hearnshaw), who helpfully taught me the rudiments of the history of British psychology, was a member of the Eugenics Society.

Note that Lewis and Eysenck had Jewish family origins. By the 1950s, the core anti-Semitism of Nazi eugenics had clearly not problematised the commitment to, and consensus about, biogenetics in the Western liberal academy.

12. P. Mazumdar (1991). *Eugenics, Human Genetics and Human Failings: The Eugenics Society, its Sources and its Critics in Britain.* London: Routledge; D. Stone (2001). Race in British eugenics. *European History Quarterly*, 1(3): 397–425.

13. My separate and book-length critique of identity politics can be found in D. Pilgrim (2022). *Identity Politics: Where Did It All Go Wrong?* Bicester: Phoenix. Note that the managers of University College London in 2020 opted to remove Galton and Pearson from their named rooms and buildings.

14. Burt took a positive interest in psychodynamic psychology. His student Eysenck was completely hostile to this possibility of rapprochement.

15. C. L. Burt (1912). The inheritance of mental characters. *Eugenic Review*, IV: 1–33; C. E. Spearman (1904). General intelligence objectively determined and measured. *American Journal of Psychology*, XV: 201–299.

16. C. L. Burt (1946). Intelligence and fertility. *Eugenics Society Occasional Papers*, Number 2; C. L. Burt (1909). Experimental tests of general intelligence. *British Journal of Psychology*, III: 94–107.

17. L. S. Hearnshaw (1979). *Cyril Burt: Psychologist.* Icatha, NY: Cornell University Press.

18. R. Fletcher (1991). *Science, Ideology and the Media: The Cyril Burt Scandal.* New Brunswick: Transaction; L. J. Kamin (1974). *The Science and Politics of IQ.* Harmondsworth: Penguin; N. J. Mackintosh (Ed.) (1995). *Cyril Burt: Fraud or Framed?* Oxford: Oxford University Press.

19. D. Pilgrim (2008). The eugenic legacy in psychology and psychiatry. *International Journal of Social Psychiatry*, 54(3): 272–284. The confident confirmatory role of concrete data for a researcher's unchecked presupposition is called the 'ontic fallacy'. The latter is a product of empiricism disabling psychologists from respecting, and being skilled at, pre-empirical and non-empirical reflection: J. Smedslund (2016). Why psychology cannot be an empirical science. *Integrative Psychological Behavioural Science*, 50(2): 185–195.

20. In common parlance, this phrase means 'prompts a fresh unanswered question'. In philosophical guidance on logic, it refers to an *unrecognised presupposition*, when making a statement. These meanings are close but not identical. Its proper use refers tightly to the risk of the ontic fallacy (see previous footnote).

21. This was the title of a popular book by H. J. Eysenck produced in 1954.
22. See D. Pilgrim, & A. Treacher (1991). *Clinical Psychology Observed*. London: Routledge; S. Morley (2000). Monte Shapiro obituary. *The Guardian*, 2 May.
23. H. J. Eysenck (1990). *Rebel with a Cause*. London: Transaction.
24. Eysenck worked at the Institute of Psychiatry in London. The latter was incorporated into King's College in 1997, hence its role in the posthumous investigation of his work.
25. A. J. Pelosi (2019). Personality and fatal diseases: revisiting a scientific scandal. *Journal of Health Psychology, 24*(4): 421–439. I am grateful to Dr Pelosi for his advice on this part of the chapter.
26. This was an early career award offered annually by the BPS. It ran from 1962 to 2020 and was 'retired' in recognition of its celebratory association with British eugenics. However, its instigation in 1962 indicates that doubts about the eugenic tradition persisted well after the Second World War. The name of the British Eugenics Society was changed to the Galton Institute in 1989.
27. Others have raised doubts about the BPS conducting a post-mortem on Eysenck's work. These doubters may be correct in practice about this futility, though in principle if his work is in such doubt, in my view it should be scrutinised fully. The question is whether the BPS has the will and competence to do this properly. See J. Hall, & A. Scarnà (2019). An aggravating controversialist or ahead of his time? *The Psychologist, 32*(5).
28. P. J. Corr (2016). The centenary of a maverick. *The Psychologist, 29*: 234–239.
29. H. B. Gibson (1981). *Hans Eysenck: The Man and His Work*. London: Peter Owens; R. Buchanan (2011). *Playing with Fire: The Controversial Career of HJ Eysenck*. Oxford: Oxford University Press.
30. R. Craig, A. Pelosi, & D. Tourish (2021). Research misconduct complaints and institutional logics: The case of Hans Eysenck and the British Psychological Society. *Journal of Health Psychology, 26*(2): 296–311; D. F. Marks (2019). The Hans Eysenck affair: Time to correct the scientific record. *Journal of Health Psychology, 24*(4): 409–420.
31. A. W. Heim (1954). *The Appraisal of Intelligence*. London: Methuen. I am grateful to Professor Anne Rogers for her information about the lesser recorded role of Heim as a challenger to the eugenic tradition, after the Second World War, in British psychometrics.
32. A. W. Heim (1971). Review of Eysenck's book 'Race Intelligence and Education'. *European Journal of Psychology, 1*(3): 404–410; cf. H. Eysenck (1972).

Race and intelligence: A reply to Alice Heim. *European Journal of Social Psychology*, *2*(2): 210–211.

33. One contradiction in Eysenck's work was that he was both a faithful bio-geneticist but also a methodological behaviourist. His work on cancer reconciled this by offering a genetic theory of causality and a version of cognitive-behavioural therapy as treatment.

34. From Shakespeare's *Hamlet*.

35. In light of the criticisms in this book, some of their titles are Orwellian and preposterous: 'Director of Communication and Engagement'; 'Change Programme Director'; 'Director of Membership, Professional Development and Standards'; and 'Director of Knowledge and Insight'.

36. Despite this fact, the CEO is designated on the BPS website as the lead contact for the BoT, signalling who is in charge (for now).

37. This refers to going inside a claim and then working outwards to reveal if it 'does what it says on the tin' in practice. This can run alongside others like an omissive critique (examining what is not said) and an explanatory critique (offering reasons why dubious claims are still sustained or believed).

CHAPTER 7

BPS bullshit

David Pilgrim

In Chapter 1, I offered a brief historical account of the emergence of the organisational crisis in the BPS. I return to the problem of developing an accurate recent history of the Society in Chapter 8. In this one, I focus on the link between organisational dysfunction in the BPS, and the norms of silence and rhetoric common in the leadership culture, which prevent such a history being properly elaborated and recorded for posterity.

We can consider two overarching causal factors, when understanding this challenge of trying to demystify the arcane world at the centre of the BPS. First, there is the structural vulnerability about a total lack of independent oversight of the organisation. Second, that structural flaw has afforded a system of governance that has gone into freefall and so has been prey to those pursuing personal power, financial gain,[1] and their particular vested interests.

Careerism and policy capture have been rewarded in that dysfunctional context and conflicts of interest have become the norm. These beneficiaries of poor governance have developed their particular forms of public rhetoric or bullshit. Those norms of mystification and dissimulation have become self-perpetuating. Thus there has been an interaction between a flawed *structure* and the deceitful *culture* of nameable actors that it has afforded.

This pattern has emerged in other organisations, not just the BPS, but it has been played out in the latter in the particular ways outlined in other chapters. The offence triggered by the dysfunctional culture prompted a critical reaction from ordinary members of the BPS—a cue for the next section.

Case study examples

When the activist group BPSWatch emerged in the autumn of 2020 (see Chapter 3), this was born of cumulative frustrations about complaints being ignored or dealt with inadequately. An early decision made was to send clear accounts of case examples to the Charity Commission. At that time, we were aware that the latter was the formal regulatory body and was already 'engaged' with the BPS about at least some of its governance 'challenges'.[2] We were also aware, on the grapevine, that the Commission was slow-moving and even, at times, ineffectual.

Accordingly, we travelled more in hope than expectation. Nonetheless, the exercise in reporting to the Commission also allowed us to organise a coherent case about the failings of the regime at the BPS, which had seemingly now entered a stage of acute crisis. Whether or not the Commission acted upon our reporting to our satisfaction was important (at this stage, we were not completely cynical about their role). However, of more importance was that we were putting on public record our case.

Until a public record is made, complainants or critics might always remain unsure about the salience and validity of their concerns. Having to turn a subjective annoyance into a case to be taken seriously by a public body focuses the mind and allows reality testing with trusted readers at the draft stage. It is also, like the blog described in Chapter 3, a way of ensuring a *historical record*, in the sure knowledge that recent and past managers in the BPS do not *want* a critical account to be recorded for the period of their regime of power.

We sent several illustrative case studies, four of which I will summarise here. In the subsequent section, I will discuss what they tell us about the dysfunctional culture in the BPS. A fifth one excluded from this chapter was about the closure of an important review group about law and memory. This is picked up in some detail by Ashley Conway in Chapter 5. The cases listed were all from verifiable named complainants, some of whom are authors in this book. However, names are not included in all cases, when and if they requested anonymity during the submission to the Commission. All of the complainants at the time of writing were longstanding BPS members and many had held senior elected office.

Case 1: Concerns about 'guidelines for psychologists working with gender, sexuality and relationship diversity'

The above document was issued by the BPS, and immediately concerns were raised about both its content and inadequacies about the process of its production. For example, psychologists offering their views as consultants at the draft stage were not sent the document before sign-off and were unhappy with many aspects of its content, with their name on it and so giving it legitimacy.

In addition to these concerns, Pat Harvey complained that the chair of the group (Dr Christina Richards) producing the guidelines had, in her public pronouncements as a psychologist, breached the Society's Code of Conduct and brought the Society into disrepute. Pat provided direct evidence in the form of video recording of Richards' public comments, and argued that the BPS had been subject to policy capture by transgender activists. She argued that the handling of her complaint was 'shockingly deficient'. It failed to follow the BPS's own written complaints procedure and was not dealt with within the time frame specified, with no explanation given.

Pat received communications from several different people, one using only their first name with no job title, signed from the anonymous 'Complaints Team'. The response cut and pasted a brief and very contentious statement published in *The Psychologist* by 'the BPS' as an answer to her complaint about deficiencies in the guidelines. The response to her complaint against the unprofessional behaviour of the chair was merely that 'the BPS is a broad church, and there will always be differing views among our members on some issues'.

Her experience followed on from the multi-signed letter about the problematic guidelines, sent to the CEO, Sarb Bajwa, on 7 June 2020. It raised serious concerns about child protection and the lack of balancing or critical arguments from the wider membership in the guidelines. This produced no response from the CEO after three weeks, and so a reminder was sent to him. He failed to reply to that reminder. The lead signatory then wrote to the then president Hazel McLaughlin on 15 September and pointed out this failure to respond from the CEO. Such a non-response was both discourteous and a dereliction of his fundamental responsibility to deal with serious matters. McLaughlin replied immediately as follows:

> Thank you for your letter today. I appreciate that you have brought this matter to my attention. I acknowledge the letter and appreciate that you have sent it previously to Sarb Bajwa in July. I have copied this email to Sarb Bajwa and to Karen Beamish. Karen has direct responsibility for membership and handles members' issues and complaints. I am asking them to respond to you on this matter. I have also copied this to David Murphy as Vice President and also a clinical psychologist by background. Please take the opportunity to liaise directly with Sarb and Karen. As President I am concerned to ensure that member's [sic] complaints are addressed and resolved in a timely manner. I look forward to hearing about the resolution on this matter.

By the end of 2020, at the time of reporting to the Charity Commission, no communication had been received from any of the above parties flagged in the message from McLaughlin.

Case 2: Concerns about extending prescribing rights to psychologists

In early October 2020, a letter signed by over a hundred psychologists was sent to Hazel McLaughlin, complaining that a move to extend prescribing rights to psychologists had emerged within the BPS as a policy. This had occurred without proper consultation with the membership. NHS England had asked whether psychologists wanted to be considered for prescribing rights, and the response, 'Yes please', had been pushed through by a partisan pro-prescribing group, which had captured the process.

The letter objected to this captured position as a 'travesty'. Objections to the principle of extending prescribing rights came from two quarters. The dominant one was from those who were resisting psychologists being drawn into biomedical interventions in mental health services. A lesser, but important contingent background, consideration was that a key figure in the pro-prescribing group was also the lead author of the controversial gender document noted above (Christina Richards). Richards supported the prescription of puberty-blockers for children, and this move about prescribing rights would then favour this political goal. Some signatories were aware of this dimension to the politics of the topic, but it was not mentioned explicitly in the letter of protest.

Thus, the letter of urgent concern came because of the imminent start of a negotiation with NHS England. Limited prescribing rights of this sort have applied to nurses for a while but because psychologists offer a *psychological* approach to healthcare, they have often been wary of its implications. That ambivalence has created schisms within the discipline as this controversy in the BPS highlights. (In the USA, there have been similar divisions about the topic, within applied psychology.[3])

Despite this fractious scenario in the discipline, with a deadline for that start of a negotiation with NHS England, McLaughlin simply treated the letter of concern (remember with *over a hundred* signatures) as a standard complaint to be processed, and she replied accordingly. The lead signatory pointed out in reply emphatically that the letter was *not* a complaint but a *request* for the BPS leadership to act urgently in order to rectify a very poor consultation and head off a premature and unfounded negotiation with the NHS.

As with the first case study above, at the centre of this concern was a highly biased group developing a policy that had ignored the voices of their critics. Again, that process had gone unchecked by officers of the Society and the Board of Trustees. Policy capture and a lack of ensured democratic debate in a purportedly learned society were afforded by weak governance. As with the first case study, by the time the report was sent to the Charity Commission, no manager in the BPS had offered an answer to the concerns from the letter writers.

A pattern was becoming clear across cases sent to the BPSWatch group: a lack of willingness or competence at the centre of the BPS to respond to legitimate concerns from members. These were either ignored, or sent into the maze of the broken complaints process indefinitely.

Case 3: Reminder to the Charity Commission of the mistreatment of recent presidents

Although the contrived expulsion of Nigel MacLennan is the grossest example of resisting governance reform from an elected president, efforts, albeit less root and branch in intention, had been obvious from others, including Jamie Hacker-Hughes and Peter Kinderman. Also note the vice president David Murphy resigned citing concerns about financial irregularities and poor governance—see Chapter 3. Kinderman, during his shortened stay as vice president, was forced to resign by the BoT; they accused him (wrongly) of fraudulent conduct.

For his part, he made a formal complaint corporately and individually against its senior officers: the chief executive (Ann Colley), the director of finance (Russell Hobbs), the honorary general secretary (Carole Allan), and the honorary treasurer (Ray Miller). (Below, I highlight that, in my view, Colley, Allan, and Miller have exemplified the oligarchical culture of the BPS.) Kinderman complained that they had frustrated the wishes of many parties in relation to a public policy matter. These included the members of the Society, the Professional Practice Board, the Divisions of Clinical and Forensic Psychology (among others) and their elected representatives, of the president and president-elect, and of significant colleagues outside the Society. The BoT had purportedly supported the latter but then deliberately failed to ensure it in practice.

This reversal was done knowingly, according to Kinderman, by the list he accused, who were in his view accordingly inept. Moreover, in the midst of this spat about decision-making and factionalism in the BoT, Kinderman reported that the named list had defamed his reputation and that of Hacker-Hughes. He also noted, in a scenario anticipating the treatment of MacLennan more recently, that discussions relevant to their role and responsibilities were held in camera by members of the BoT and that they were denied relevant audit reports.

I have summarised here a complex scenario that was passed in more elaborate form in our bundle to the Charity Commission. This had a double significance because it strengthened our reporting of a pattern of misgovernance, but at the same time it pointed up that the Charity Commission *itself* was unresponsive. Kinderman had made all the above points to the Commission in 2018 but he had received no reply from them. This seems to point up a cross-organisational cultural tendency, which is to resist corrective feedback, by simply ignoring matters that are too problematic to resolve.

Case 4: Censorship and contempt for freedom of expression

In September 2019, I had a piece published in the ethics column of the *Division of Clinical Psychology Forum*, raising serious moral questions for practitioners in relation to the transgender controversy (see case study #1 above). Over the years, I had written several pieces for the ethics column (a product of my interest in the philosophy, as well as the history, of psychology). They had been well received and editors had invited new pieces from me. Like the others, this was not a polemic or casual opinion piece. It adopted standard philosophical arguments, appropriate to our shared current social context, about an important matter of public interest and for clinical practice.

This led to a letter of complaint about the piece from the Tavistock Clinic, which the editor was *instructed* to print by a member of the SMT (not named to me), overriding the normal convention of editorial control and independence. Correspondence from me in response, to be printed by the editor (with his agreement), was also censored by an anonymous BPS staff member. I complained to the BPS about this interference in academic freedom, but no apology was issued to me or the editor. No account was given to us of who had made the decision and why.

This frustrating scenario prompted me to reflect on the question of freedom of expression *itself* as an ethical matter, as well as whether the BPS was now more preoccupied with PR than intellectual integrity.

Accordingly, I submitted another piece, which detailed why, in my view, academic freedom was in jeopardy in the Society. The editor made minor edits and then agreed that this second piece would indeed be published. At all times, he acted supportively and properly, but his decisions were clearly being overridden by the concerns of the 'Comms Team'. The agreed article did not go into print.

When I asked why the piece had not appeared, the chair of the Division of Clinical Psychology (a trustee) assured me by email that this was a Covid-created delay. When it still failed to appear after several months, I wrote to the CEO explaining my concerns, as well as to the vice president, David Murphy. They shepherded me into the black hole of the complaints process. It disappeared without trace, though I subsequently put the piece, in full, on the BPSWatch.com blog.

I continued to demand an explanation for why the piece was not published and was told that this was because of its poor quality (no person was named making this judgement). This was simply not true: the editor was happy with it and wanted it to be published.[4] This was a case of censorship, plain and simple, by an anonymous BPS apparatchik.

With persistence, I managed to establish the identity of the investigatory officer who examined my complaint that the article had been censored. It was the CEO, Sarb Bajwa, who had sent it into the complaints process in the first place and had not offered me any principled view about protecting academic freedom. He upheld the view that the piece was not published for reasons of poor quality (repeated here for emphasis, ignoring the view of the editor who wanted the piece to appear).

I never discovered who exactly imposed this censorship; that information was refused me. Had I not complained repeatedly about the censorship, I would never have even discovered the role of Mr Bajwa as the 'investigatory officer'. By that time, he was suspended, and so his decision must have predated November 2020. I secured the information about his role nearly a year later, after my repeated demands.[5]

This case study exposes both the acceptability of censorship in the current BPS culture and the secretive, mystifying, and broken complaints system. (I am not special pleading here about an unusual circumstance: I was one of many of its victims.) The concerns of the 'Comms

Team' for PR and spin, or what Erving Goffman called 'impression management',[6] are a cue for the next section.

Charity Commission passivity and BPS bullshit

At the time of writing, none of the matters we (the BPSWatch group) raised with the Charity Commission have been dealt with to our satisfaction. Note Peter Kinderman's failure to receive any response from the Commission. Such 'non-events' reflect a lacklustre performance from a body existing purportedly to protect the public in its role of surveillance and correction about charitable bodies. To date, the Commission have claimed to remain 'engaged' with the BPS about its failures of governance but have not moved towards a full statutory investigation or take it into direct management or 'special measures'. This indolent passivity really does not inspire confidence. At present, it seems to me that we may have to wait for other more efficient forms of legal or journalistic investigation to reveal, for the full public record, the extent and detailed content of organisational failure in the BPS.

Turning to the implications of that organisational failure, one important starting point is its structural vulnerability, which has been alluded to in previous pages. The basic fault or foundational flaw of the BPS is that it simply has no independent oversight to ensure that what it claims about *any* matter, whether it is public policy or academic integrity, is actualised. That lack of oversight then sets up the conditions of possibility for chaos, inefficiency, conflicts of interest, policy capture by groups of activists, the betrayal of academic values, and eventually simple corruption. The policy capture tendency is explored in Chapters 4 and 5.

To be clear here, I am not arguing that a properly constituted independent Board of Trustees, alongside a proper complaints process that commands the respect of complainants, would magically solve all of the problems of a complex organisation. They are necessary but not sufficient, but note, *they are necessary*. Until that structural reform, the sorry symptom checklist of misgovernance, just described, will continue. Moreover, persistent secrecy and bullshit will preoccupy the leadership.

Bullshit: everything said and not said for the powerful to remain powerful

'Bullshit' creates squeamishness for some people. As a mild swear word, it is sometimes euphemised as 'BS'. However, it has been incorporated into mainstream social science as a vehicle for the analysis of deceitfulness in public life. In that role, it was popularised by Harry Frankfurt.[7] He did not invent the term. However, he documented its history and adopted, and capitalised upon, its shoot-from-the-hip value.

In America, 'horseshit' is also sometimes used, and in Britain (especially in military settings) there is the shorter term 'bull'. In Australia, we also find 'bull dust', and in English slang the word 'bollocks' is equivalent and more common (as in 'you are talking bollocks' or 'what a load of bollocks'). This resistance, from below, to the rhetoric of those in power reminds us of the insight from 1939 by W. C. Fields that 'you can't cheat an honest man'.[8]

Bullshit connotes deceit but it is different from the narrower notion of lying. In the latter case, the liar knows what the truth is and seeks to avoid the consequences of its confession. In this sense, those lying, and those lied to, are both part of the same field of truth, but play different roles within it. For example, the apprehended criminal knows what breaking the law means all too well and then opts if accused (validly) to deny his or her involvement. By contrast, the bullshitter is indifferent to the truth; their main concern is to sustain an impression that suits their interests contingently. If that means lying or telling the truth and all stops in between, as long as it works to their advantage, then that is what matters.

Bullshit is then a comprehensive strategy of pretence: whatever it takes to maintain a preferred view of reality, just do it. It can entail lies or truths and extensive emollient rhetoric or strategic silence. In politics, it invites recurring in-jokes about being 'economical with the truth'.[9] The con artist celebrates this talent, but bullshit can also generalise to become a group norm and even cultural tendency. Increasingly, with the growth of managerialism, organisational researchers have noted the latter. 'Management speak' with confident terminology and phrases abound, and many employees now simply expect their managers to talk bullshit.[10] Clichés are offered, as and when required, to mollify the public. When the latter are assured about probity, transparency, or safety in a press release, then there are often good grounds for healthy suspicion from the ordinary citizen.

When we consider bullshit in the context of organisational culture, rather than individual impression management, it requires group loyalty to a line of reasoning or an opted collective silence on a particular matter. For example, on our blog, we have posted extensive attacks on the BoT and the SMT, at times pointedly noting individual failings. And yet, no one from those two groups has responded publicly to us, even though we know that they have silently monitored both the blog and its attached Twitter account (see Chapter 3).[11] This suggests a strategic decision to evade public exposure by not trading accounts with us, presumably with the hope that we will not be noticed or, even better, disappear without trace. 'Engagement' with critics might pose a risk of exposing the very problems that they wish to keep secret in the public domain.

Thus we can think of the costs of a bullshit culture in two senses. The funds of the organisation are spent directly on management self-protection and PR, but also there are *opportunity costs*. Managers spend their time bullshitting instead of simply doing the job described on the BPS website. For example, why did the CEO, Sarb Bajwa, not reply to letters from members about serious matters—did he not have the time? He did have the time to raise concerns with the 'trustees' that he was having to deal with too many complaints from members. In any well-functioning organisation, complaints would be welcomed learning points for quality improvement. The fact that the BPS is not a well-functioning organisation accounts for the CEO's understandable need for a quiet life, uninterrupted by members' feedback.

During that period (2020 up to November, when he was suspended), the CEO spent time on another form of diversionary activity, aligned with this point about bullshit and its opportunity costs. Every month in *The Psychologist* there was a column setting out his wisdom. This habit petered out after his suspension, though no explanation was printed by the editor. However, because of publication set-up times, his contributions still appeared after November 2020.

My point here is not to analyse the ideological cogency of the *content* of the CEO's column but, instead, to draw attention to a functional *process*. This came with the mere semiotic presence of the CEO, pictured smartly dressed and smiling. It signalled benign parental authority, a safe pair of hands, and a commitment to organisational probity. All was well with the world of the BPS. The CEO was taking time out of his very busy schedule to share his authoritative thoughts with the readers.

Although his column disappeared in early 2021, his deputy Diane Ashby, appointed primarily to be the lead for the controversial £6 million 'Change Programme', did not replace him as a writer. This non-event was meaningful: how would she have accounted for her own sudden appearance in *The Psychologist*? What content might be effective to deflect the readers' attention from the actualities of the crisis?

The answers to these questions, to say the least, were tricky. A low profile was probably wise from the perspective of an SMT understandably fearing that a cat might soon be out of the bag (and amongst the pigeons) in relation to the large fraud. With that would come the yet to be explored question about the oversight responsibilities of the SMT and the BoT. Also, what about the disintegration of the presidential triumvirate and the controversial expulsion of Nigel MacLennan in particular? Two elected presidents resigned and one was expelled in the space of just two months in 2021, when Mr Bajwa was on paid absence. 'Least said, soonest mended', Ms Ashby probably thought and hoped. Bullshit is about silence, not just emollient rhetoric.[12]

Silence in *The Psychologist* indeed prevailed until Bajwa returned at the end of 2021. The membership were told that it had been a 'challenging year'[13] but, very conveniently, no details were offered. We were also told that the Society was at 'a crossroads', but told nothing about what the signpost pointing in different directions actually said. The game of hide and seek, with its mixture of silence and rhetoric, blandishments and safe pieties, faux-humility and bombast, was at its height in 2021.

Pollyanna management in a 'Psychological' Society

Organisational bullshit is thus complex stuff. It has the general features just described, but also ones that are inflected in their concrete singularity, case by case. And in the case of the BPS, it takes on an almost surreal quality at times because it is, after all, allegedly a *Psychological* Society.

Any sceptical critique, put forward by the contributors to this book, can be contrasted with the rhetorical aspirations from those running the organisation, with their supportive cast and chorus of ambivalent presidents and biddable appointed trustees. As for the ineffectual neutered senate, with no terms of reference, it offers ordinary BPS members and the public zero confidence. Note again, the BPS has not a *single* independent trustee or senate member to say when the emperor is naked. The surfeit of conflicts of interest endemic to the BPS culture ensures this scenario of collusive pretence.

In 2015, with an earnest foreword from the then president Dorothy Miell, the BPS issued its *Strategic Plan 2015–2020*. This can be found immediately and free online by the public. The whole document warrants an exercise in extensive critical discourse analysis, but here I note just a few relevant points. At the outset, it says this:

> Our values are central to the way we work to achieve our core purposes. We aim to work in a culture of:
>
> - rigour and fairness;
> - honesty and integrity;
> - transparency;
> - respect for a diversity of viewpoints;
> - the highest standards of professionalism and ethical behaviour, attitudes and judgements, as laid out in our Code of Ethics and Conduct.

There is obviously nothing wrong with these aspirations, when they are read in the abstract. However, when and if they are used as a bullshit checklist, then they leave the BPS exposed to ridicule. Laudable aspirations cannot be gainsaid. Wish lists, which pay no attention to honesty about a present reality or the disturbing crimes and misdemeanours inherited from the past, produce a vacuous meringue. The latter is all form and no substance, and its pretty outer shell *is* the bullshit. I return to these important criteria of probity in Chapter 8.

The report endorsed by Miell was revisited by the new president, Katherine Carpenter, who was imported to replace Nigel MacLennan for a year. By the end of 2021, Carpenter was pinning her hopes on the 'New Strategic Framework' and inviting members into a bright shiny future. Forget the past and leap off the fiery hot coals of the present to the ambient temperature of a future idyll.

We can see then that, faced with the dire state of the BPS, one after another president has had some tough choices. The simplest answer for a quiet life, and their enhanced CV status, was to play their own biddable part in the BPS bullshit generator. Illustrative examples here would be Ray Miller, Ann Colley, and Carole Allan. Their collective narrative was of long service as a *self-evident virtue*, not one in which their regime of power shielded the Society from robust democratic scrutiny.

Miller was president of the Society in 2006. Apart from this role, he has also at various points been chair of the Division of Clinical Psychology and chair of the Professional Practice Board. He was honorary treasurer of the BPS (2013–2019) and was a trustee for thirteen years. (It is considered poor practice for trustees in charities to serve more than a few years before leaving their role.) In conversation with the then CEO Tim Cornford in 2006, he described himself, very honestly and fairly, as being a 'BPS junkie' since 1984 (*The Psychologist*, 2006).

Turning to Ann Colley, she was unique as both a CEO for a while and also BPS president. This was printed in *The Psychologist* about Colley in 2017, when she was retiring from the role of CEO. It was an appreciation from another ex-president, Carole Allan, herself now the honorary general secretary of the Society:[14]

> Ann served[15] twice as Honorary General Secretary. The first time was for three years from 1989, when membership of the Society stood at 13,000. The second time was from 2003 to 2008. In between she was elected to serve as President, which office she held in 1993/94. Ann was circumspect about what Presidents can achieve in their short term of office when she was interviewed for *The Psychologist*, pointing out that initiatives usually only bear fruit after two or three years.[16]

Not all presidents were as tentative in their expectations about change as Colley, who, like Miller, was clearly a 'BPS junkie'.[17] For example, Peter Kinderman and Jamie Hacker-Hughes saw the governance problems and tried to tinker, and they were soon punished. Those like MacLennan were bolder, as he signalled his reformist intentions even before he was elected in his candidate statement.

Conclusion

This chapter has extended the points made in Chapter 3 about why an alternative account to that preferred by BPS officialdom (in *The Psychologist* and its other publications) is required if we are to provide a valid and fair history of the Society. The structural vulnerability to misgovernance traceable to 1988, with its missed opportunity for a fresh start with genuinely independent trustees, was noted in Chapter 1 and thereafter. Any confession to, or exposure of, the misgovernance that inevitably followed threatened the interests of those with contingent power. This then created the conditions of possibility for a culture of organisational bullshit. For students of dysfunctional organisations, the BPS offers itself, for now, as an ideal case study.

Notes

1. Apart from the salaries to the SMT and those lower in the bureaucratic hierarchy (over a hundred employees), there has been a tradition of paying the (appointed, not elected) honorary secretary of the BPS a substantial honorarium. This sinecure payment was stopped in recent years. However, because of the opaqueness of the Society, I have been unable to identify who made this decision, when, and why. I am grateful, though, to ex-president David Murphy for relaying this (albeit imprecise) picture to me by email.
2. These terms are placed in quotation marks to indicate that they are common management speak. This is relevant given the chapter title.
3. At the time of writing, five states in the USA have given prescribing rights to psychologists, but it remains controversial within the discipline; see: prescriptive-authority.pdf (apaservices.org)
4. I have an email trail to confirm this pattern of events about the censorship of my article.
5. By 2021, my challenging emails to the SMT were becoming so frequent that Ms Ashby accused me of harassing BPS staff. She pointed up the dignity at

work policy and instructed her colleagues not to reply to me about any matter any more. This continued the theme of Mr Bajwa in the previous year, asking the BoT how he could stop members making so many complaints.

6. This term is well known in social psychology (E. Goffman (1959). *The Presentation of Self in Everyday Life*. New York: Override).

7. H. Frankfurt (2005). *On Bullshit*. Princeton, NJ: Princeton University Press. See also L. T. Christensen, D. Kärreman, & A. Rasche (2019). Bullshit and organization studies. *Organization Studies*, 40(10): 1587–1600; N. Hardy (2021). Catcher in the lie: Resisting *bovine ordure* in social epistemology. *Journal of Critical Realism*, 20(2): 125–145.

   Given the post-truth society enabled and sacralised by the Trump presidency, we are all now embedded in a culture where deceitfulness has become the norm. For a critique of this tendency since the postmodern turn, see B. Williams (2002). *Truth and Truthfulness*. Princeton, NJ: Princeton University Press.

8. Of course, in the psychodynamic tradition it is assumed that we all are dishonest with ourselves and one another on a daily basis. We might then think of bullshit as a conveniently adaptive mixture of rationalisations and denials, elevated within the speech community of managers to a 'skill set'. In that sense, the language of individual psychopathology is insufficient because there is an *emergent cultural norm* of deceit; A. Spicer (2020). Playing the bullshit game: How empty and misleading communication takes over organizations. *Organization Theory*, 1: 1–26

9. https://en.wikipedia.org/wiki/Economical_with_the_truth

10. Many managers know they are involved (for varying amounts of their time) in the bullshit game noted by Spicer above. Those more captivated by it tend to have no insight or sense of irony about their working lives. They believe in their own bullshit. I once attended a workshop run by Robert Hare on psychopathy. An early stock question he asks is for people to write down a psychopath who they know at present; one of the commonest responses Hare recorded was 'my boss'. See R. P. Boddy, R. Ladysjewsky, & P. L. Galvin (2010). Leaders without ethics in global business: Corporate psychopaths. *Journal of Public Affairs*, 10(1): 131–138; B. J. Board, & K. Fritzon (2005). Disordered personalities at work. *Psychology, Crime and Law*, 11(1): 17–32; P. Babiak, & R. D. Hare (2007). *Snakes in Suits: When Psychopaths go to Work*. New York: HarperCollins.

11. We have had just a few email protests about our campaign from the BPS SMT. They have accused us of harassing BPS staff and violating a dignity at work policy (see note 4 above). This is another small example of bullshit.

12. This silence was broken online in December 2021, after Bajwa came back from his year of suspension, as the journalistic cliché goes, to 'take control of the narrative'. He and Katherine Carpenter set out a long and confident piece in the ever-biddable magazine of the British Psychological Society, *The Psychologist*. It outlined a bright future with not a single allusion to the serious political mess witnessed in the recent past. Instead, the only challenge implied was about the organisational and social implications of Covid-19. See https://thepsychologist.bps.org.uk/volume-35/january-2022/president-and-chief-executive?dm_i=6MRE,ELU5,3OHQ7J,1RE4W,1

13. This 'challenging year' semantic wriggle was found in the statement from Bajwa noted in the previous endpoint. Clever in its vagueness, it has the hallmark of an advised Comms Team 'party line'. Also, it has allowed those in power to play victim and seek sympathy and support from BPS members, while conveniently keeping them in the dark about precise details. The same semantic wriggle was used in the unrepentant statement from Carol McGuinness in her ill-advised YouTube piece, the text of which is still on record: C. McGuinness (2021). The Society is at a crossroads. *The Psychologist*, *34*: 4–5.

14. Allan was BPS president 2011–2012. She went on to become honorary general secretary, retiring from the role in 2021.

15. That single word 'served' is open to substantial discussion, in the view of the critics of the BPS. *Who* was being served—the public and membership? *What* was being served—transparency and democracy?

16. 'Always cheerful and positive', *The Psychologist* (bps.org.uk).

17. *The Psychologist* (2006). *Double top—Ray Miller in discussion with Tim Cornford: The Society's new President in discussion with the Chief Executive. How do their roles work together, and where do they see the Society going?* April, *19*, 20–21.

CHAPTER 8

What is the purpose of the BPS?

David Pilgrim

In this final substantive chapter, I begin with what sociologists call 'interest work'. Today, the BPS is a bureaucracy that represents the interests of psychology as a modern discipline in the academy. In addition, it also represents applied psychologists and purports to act in the public interest. Moreover, under the regime of neoliberalism extant since the 1980s, there has been the compromise of the 'new public management' model, which has permeated the public and third-sector structures of Western capitalism. Accordingly, we need to be mindful of an emergent interest group, which comprises career managers and their subordinate administrative staff.

Thus, what starts as a very obvious point (that any organisation reflects egotistical interests and interest groups) leads quite quickly to a reflection on their range and their implicit or explicit intentions and aspirations. An attention to interests (plural) is a necessity if we are to grasp in a fair manner: the current functioning of the BPS; where that has arisen from; and the imagined futures of the organisation to consider.

Maybe there are winners and losers in the power struggles that ensue from discrepant interests within any organisation. Many of the points made in previous chapters would suggest this is the case in the BPS. And with those power struggles, there are casualties, including the casualty of truth. By the latter, I mean the constraints that are now evident about transparency (leaving ordinary members and the general public in the dark or mystified). Again, the previous chapters, *inter alia*, have addressed this matter of truth suppression, mystification, and bullshit, which for now characterise the culture at the centre of the BPS.

The conditions of possibility for a proper history of the BPS

Although in my previous chapters I have flagged the difficulties in offering a critical history of the BPS, more can be said here. A good starting point is the fragility of the History and Philosophy Section of the Society, which I know well (as its current honorary general secretary and past chair). Despite its name, it is new in the context of the existence of the Society itself. It emerged over ninety years after the formation of the latter. In the interim period until today, the Section has been kept going by a few stalwarts with a particular interest in the words in its title.[1] At the end of the chapter, I will return to the evidence of recent constraints on the potentially illuminative role of the Section about the BPS and its lacklustre past.

In light of the points I raised in Chapter 1, organised psychology in the twentieth century was not a propitious context to encourage an interest in either history or philosophy. Taking these one by one, the first has tended to be demoted in importance by positivism and the fetish this creates about up-to-date evidence. The second has resonances of a past and resented parent. The naïve realism offered by Ward and Rivers in their rhetorical stall-setting in the first editorial of the *British Journal of Psychology* encouraged a preoccupation with up-to-date facts.

The latter still is the obsession today of modern psychology and is reflected in the aims encouraged in the undergraduate curriculum. However, as I noted in Chapter 1, that positivist cultural tendency was disrupted by the postmodern turn and the discipline incorporating arguments about perspectivism. This led to a major (though not often recognised) historical compromise for the discipline: methodologism.

That compromise allowed the discipline (and note also therefore the cultural tendency inside the BPS) to appear to hold together psychologists with highly discrepant theoretical and methodological concerns. That containment in the BPS is reflected in the corridors of both academic psychology departments and those existing in professional settings. The collective noun of a 'disagreement of psychologists' might be a weak witticism, but it has pointed up a serious ontological point: it is what actually characterises academic and applied psychology today.

Critical and celebratory histories

Faced with that current confusion about the character of psychology as a discipline today, we can approach a history of the BPS via two main routes. The first is celebratory and the second critical. The first has a conservative rhetorical value for disciplinary leaders. It sets out the worthiness of those kick-starting the discipline and its growing liberation from the dominance of philosophy, on one side, and medicine, on the other, which I introduced in Chapter 1. That good news story can then be expanded by the notion of scientific incrementalism: as the years rolled by, the modern corpus of psychological knowledge and applied expertise just got better all the time.

By contrast, critical histories query that picture and explore rhetorical and theoretical incoherence, when faced with the complexities of human conduct and experience in varying contexts across time and space. This has ensured epistemological pluralism, with theoretical incommensurability. It has culminated, as I noted in Chapter 1, in a narrow but fragile consensus, just noted, about 'methodologism' in the discipline, reflected in the claim from the BPS that it is a 'broad church'.

Those complexities imply the need to be sceptical about interest work and the particular rhetoric of justification,[2] which psychologists might use in pursuit of their own statuses, salaries, and theoretical or professional preferences. (Recently, I have examined the difference between celebratory and critical histories of psychology elsewhere.[3])

At the end of the chapter, I explain my pessimism that it is possible for us to apply that need for a sceptical historical approach in the BPS, given its current command and control organisational culture. Before reaching that conclusion, I will summarise the catalogue of organisational failures evident in the BPS. Such a catalogue, if taken seriously as a valid description, warrants an exploration of antecedents, and that would need to be critical. By contrast, a celebratory history would be complicit with the conservative claims made today by leaders in the BPS, which are dutifully reported in its house magazine *The Psychologist*. We have given several examples of this trend in previous chapters.

Organisational dysfunction as an immediate impediment to a critical history of the BPS

Given the large cultural gap between the turns of the twentieth and twenty-first centuries, it is impossible for the BPS to be today what it started out to be. The question is whether it is organisationally capable of surviving in that new context. The evidence we have offered in the earlier chapters suggests that it has survived but has done so in a highly dysfunctional way.

In light of the problems we have highlighted, and with reference to Graham Buchanan's summary of optimal organisational leadership in Chapter 2, we might ask if a history (celebratory or critical) of the BPS even matters. We could move immediately to offer advice or prescriptions for organisational change. Indeed, below I will summarise how the recent evidence of dysfunction could be a simple checklist for that exercise of organisational rescue. However, there are two wider matters to consider about the social and historical context of the crisis clearly facing the BPS. Without their consideration, we will fail to understand where the BPS came from and where it might go.

The first is that the original rationale for the BPS announced in 1904 by Ward and Rivers emerged in a simpler and smaller disciplinary world. They offered us a reassuring version of scientism. This advocated chasing facts, in a de-contextualised way, about human functioning by mimicking laboratory physics and obsessing about David Hume's (dubious) confidence in 'constant conjunctions' between two variables (correlational studies). This allegedly would generate 'disinterested' knowledge about human conduct and experience across time and space (empirical invariance). This was a false trail because human systems are open and fluxing, and science, especially human science, cannot be value-neutral.

The breakdown in legitimacy of this simplistic programme, in the wake of Popperian and post-Popperian critiques, from the philosophy of science, now make that project implausible. Moreover, disciplinary unity of purpose was feasible only with small numbers. That advantage of small scale was eroded more and more after the Second World War as the BPS expanded. This triggered its fragmentation, evidenced by the emergence of the ACP, AEP, and the ABP.

The second contextual point is that organised intellectual labour, typified in a wide range of academic interest groups during the twentieth century, separately cannot offer the general public and public policy-makers tenable advice. Those uni-disciplinary interest groups may wish to *claim* that this is possible, when competing for influence. However, it is clear that the major problems facing us today are complex and warrant not just multi-disciplinary cooperation but also the production of true trans-disciplinary knowledge. This leaves the role of uni-disciplinary organisations, like the BPS (amongst many), offering the public an implausible form of special pleading. Flipping from one version of uni-disciplinary dominance to another provides no credible solution.

An example of this is the fate of the long-running Radio 4 programme *All in the Mind*. The discourse of this was driven for many years by its chairing *psychiatrists*. However, eventually it was taken over by a journalist-cum-*psychologist* and the BPS 'Comms Team' became increasingly adept at feeding stories, which expanded the reputation of psychology at the expense of the older medical dominance. Moreover, storylines about CBT and mindfulness being a solution to all personal or even social problems were aligned with a culture of narcissism, neoliberalism, and identity politics. Today, the rhetoric of unending forms of warranted individualism ('because you're worth it') have made psychology a very popular subject to study and to consume as clients in applied settings.

Guidance from the relevant published literature

The organisational psychology and management studies literature is a useful benchmark to make sense of problems in the BPS. Over and above the leadership literature summarised in Chapter 2, we can also look at what we expect from an optimally functioning organisation today and what we know from the literature about those that are dysfunctional. Poorly managed and governed organisations tend to have five key features:[4]

- An *absence of trust* between those managing the organisation.
- A fear of conflict that might reveal challenges in the organisation that need to be addressed. *Artificial harmony* is confected and constructive debate avoided.
- A lack of genuine personal commitment: there is a *feigned buy-in* to (questionable) group decisions, which risks the creation of ambiguity and mystification across the organisation.
- *Personal accountability is evaded,* and peers and superiors are not challenged about their conduct when required. This leads to a drop in standards of both efficiency and probity in the organisation.
- There is an *inattention to systemic success* and prioritisation of individual manager performance or status. The ego inflation of individual managers dominates and team success in the interest of stated organisation goals is backgrounded.

Reading earlier chapters in this book will persuade the reader that the BPS seems to be a classic case of a dysfunctional organisation according to these five criteria. The description by Pat Harvey, in Chapter 3, of members being kept in the dark is of particular relevance to the case of the BPS, where members themselves might hold relevant competences and knowledge about organisational improvement. Instead, the latter have been systematically excluded by poor managers, even though there is a relevant literature that good managers should know about and deploy about good communication and their personal duties of due diligence in this regard.[5]

What the BPS culture has manifested instead, which encourages the poor communication and the norms of bullshit production I noted in Chapter 7, has been a lack of clear objectives and poor governance (or oversight). In particular, the priorities set in the organisation have been on the freedom of managers to do their own thing in their own time and on their own terms. To succeed in this manager-centred strategy, the ordinary members and their legitimate knowledge, which would be of genuine utility to the organisation, have had to be systematically excluded.

There has been a self-perpetuating cultural norm of top-down closed-system management, which has kept ordinary members unaware and democratically excluded. These 'norm circles' within the organisation have involved old oligarchs dominating decision-making and then socialising new leaders, appointed or elected, into their pre-ferred forms of custom and practice. This has created what we might call disparagingly a 'cabal', but even a more neutral term would still subsume the cultural point being made. It is those cultural norm circles and processes of socialisation that are at issue in a self-perpetuating dysfunctional organisation.

The cabal culture has been one of command and control, with managers seeking compliance from members in voluntary roles in the sub-systems. That need to seek compliance, combined with keeping members in the dark, have characterised an organisation that has pri-oritised the needs of its leaders (the old oligarchs and the new manag-ers) and subordinated the rights and roles of ordinary members to that prioritisation. Such a culture of command and control is antithetical to developing an organisation that is personally inclusive and respect-ful of the qualities and expectations of a graduate membership, much of which is highly credentialised. That membership may have expected support and respect from the centre of the BPS. What they have actually encountered is disrespect and manipulation.[6]

Good managers should mediate sensitively a balance between the level of organisational compliance necessitated on pragmatic grounds, and the level of personal respect and democratic inclusion expected in a membership organisation. That balance has clearly been missing in the BPS. Instead, the needs of the leaders (see checklist above of five crite-ria of a dysfunctional organisation) have ensured that rigid bureaucratic norms have subverted good organisational performance and ethical pro-bity.[7] If BPS leaders have had insight into this failure, then they have not admitted this to the world (as the Korn Ferry Report made very clear).

Moreover, that lack of insight has been manifest in the clear lack of competence in the management culture in producing a trustworthy and efficient culture (cf. the five criteria of dysfunction noted above). A trusting, democratic, inclusive membership organisation should demonstrate recognition and gratitude from managers to members, working as volunteers in the sub-systems. Those managers have created the very opposite organisational scenario. They have been allowed to do so because of the absence of oversight (i.e., the absence of a truly inde-pendent Board of Trustees).

Note then the toxic interaction of the absence of a needed public scrutiny and oversight (displaced by the faux Board of Trustees) and the career opportunism from the old oligarchy and the new managers. With that failure, there have been decrements of both efficiency and ethical performance predicted from the literature.[8] Those oligarchs (or 'BPS junkies') have been routinely complicit in both of these facets of organisational dysfunction. Moreover, the proven link in organisations between the level of democratic involvement and transactional success, or performance, has been evident in the BPS.[9]

Constraints on a critical account of organisational failure

Here, I return then to a challenge noted earlier. If, as the authors in this book have argued, the BPS is in dire straits, as a credible fit-for-purpose membership organisation with charitable status, can members occupying the relevant sub-systems reflect critically upon that scenario? I alluded to those in the History and Philosophy Section being in a difficult position, if they wanted to offer a critical rather than a celebratory account.

Also, the beneficiaries of the recent history of dysfunction (and corruption) in the BPS continue to lead it and would be exposed to criticism about their liability if such an account were to emerge. Some ex-presidents and board members have a legacy liability that might be exposed if their dirty linen were to be washed in public. Thus, many current and past leaders of the BPS have a vested interest in silence about the past or, if needed, they would prefer the safe blandishments emerging from a celebratory history.

This book is being produced outside of the organisation, and so we can offer an uncompromising critique in its pages. By contrast, with my insider hat on as a BPS member, I would not be confident that my critical claims and sentiments would be printed in material published by the Society itself. Those doubts have been raised by several experiences I have had in relation to trying, as an insider, to bring a critical perspective to bear on the work of the organisation.

For example, my experience of being censored by someone (still to be named) inside the BPS was described in Chapter 6. My attempts to complain about this fundamental violation of freedom of expression in a purportedly learned Society culminated in failure. However, I did discover that the dismissive investigating officer was the chief executive. He clearly then considered that censorship was acceptable and, from his vantage point of interest work, this is quite understandable.

Another example of my conclusion that critical thought is not welcomed in the organisation came from two attempts on my part to put myself forward for membership of important policy groups. One was in relation to poverty, and the other the re-launched memory and law group. In the first instance, my CV provided clear evidence that I had published extensively in this field, in relation to social class and mental health, in the past thirty years.[10] I offered the additional potential advantage to the group of also being a sociologist, who had co-authored a prestigious award-winning book in the field of the sociology of mental health. I was told in the rejection letter that others who were 'more suitably qualified' were appointed. When I spoke subsequently to one member of the group, she was extremely perplexed about my exclusion, given my relevant reputation.

In the case of the memory and law group, like the author of Chapter 5, Ashley Conway, I received a similar rationale of rejection (that others more suitable were appointed). This was despite me writing a recent book of central relevance which argued that the focus on false positive decision-making in the field of child sexual abuse was placing children at risk. That distorted decision-making has been supported by the pre-existing report from the BPS in this field and reported in Chapter 5. Ashley Conway, at the end of that chapter, provides the reader with a typical example of how the centre of the BPS claims to respect and proffer transparency as a key value, but blatantly does the very opposite.

In another example and very recently, I had written on behalf of the committee of the History and Philosophy Section to express our concerns that the conclusion of the Korn Ferry Report, about the alienation between ordinary members and the BPS leadership, remained a challenge. I drew specific attention to the lack of transparency in decision-making about the future of the History of Psychology Centre and its staffing.

Pre-Covid-19, I had been involved in a working group guiding this trajectory. Our advice was ignored by the leaders of the BPS or used selectively and without telling the group of managerial intentions. I discovered that both the chief executive and the director of knowledge and insight had indeed been active, doing as they wished about the matter, but they had not engaged with the group. Indeed, the director of knowledge and insight reported her activity to the Research Board unashamedly and as a matter of fact. It transpired that the chair of our group who was appointed (an ex-president) had had some meetings with the SMT but she had not reported their content to members of the working group, nor had she re-convened our group despite repeated requests.

The chair of the Research Board responded to our letter of complaint, making no concessions to the problems of democracy and transparency we were highlighting, in the wake of the sensitising conclusion of the critical Korn Ferry Report. He did say he would raise our concerns with the Board of Trustees (as an appointed member of that faux board). At the time of writing, no reply has been forthcoming. The trend of a 'Problem? What problem?' response from the centre of the BPS, discussed in Chapter 3, was evident once more in this casual dismissal of seriously expressed concerns from ordinary members, who were volunteers in a sub-system.

The last of these scenarios, signalling the wariness of the BPS leader-ship to ever respond properly and in the spirit of being a learning organ-isation to critical feedback, is an ideal example of the challenge that anyone inside the BPS has in instigating organisational improvement. Accordingly, the prospect of, say, members of the History and Philoso-phy Section being permitted to offer a critical history of the Society in any of its publications is, in my view, very low and probably zero.

If that conclusion is fair and valid, then we are facing an organisa-tion that is not only dysfunctional but is not a learned Society, despite its rhetoric. It will remain, as I noted in Chapter 6, as an 'organisation without a memory'. If history is encouraged at all, it will probably be either celebratory or, if critical, it will deal with miscreants who are now safely dead and gone (such as Hans Eysenck).[11] This has a rhetori-cal advantage, liked by managers within their current regime of power. They can say 'that was then but this is now, and now is absolutely fine'.

Conclusion

In response to the question posed in the title of this chapter, my answer is necessarily nuanced and even contradictory. If we answer it in terms of some interest groups, then it has succeeded—it does indeed have a purpose. For example, currently it provides highly paid employment to a management class, which has no obligated interest in psychology as a discipline, or the protection of traditional academic values. It has also served the CVs and careers of BPS leaders (employed, elected, or appointed) well. Consultants and lawyers appointed to serve their interests have also been beneficiaries, at times, of the financial resources of the BPS. Those who have profited corruptly and illegally on the margins of this 'cash cow', kept alive by membership fees, might also be considered in this mix.

If we look to the BPS to embrace interdisciplinary cooperation in the public interest, then like other uni-disciplinary organisations, it has failed. There is no political justification for *any* individual discipline to claim a privileged role in the production of public policy. The examples I gave of the policy groups on poverty and memory and the law exemplify this cultural trope of disciplines over-selling their worth in the public interest, while lacking self-doubt or self-criticism. Psychology is not peculiar in this regard, but it does replicate the pattern of special pleading from a narrow epistemological base. Given that base in this case is so contested and at times confused, there are particular grounds for wariness from the general public and from policy-makers.

If we expect the centre of the organisation to be transparent in the public interest, then the BPS has clearly failed. Likewise, if we expect it to be a democratically inclusive organisation on behalf of its fee-paying members, then it has failed. Arguably these dismal outcomes do offer a positive purpose (in relation to the query in my title): the BPS provides an immediate and perfectly formed example of a dysfunctional organisation for students in management schools.

The Society may have failed the public and its members, but that case study may still have its pedagogical use. This, though, is an unintended consequence of the biased forms of interest work operating in an organisation that has lacked public accountability. The structural flaw underpinning this dysfunctional culture has emerged and been maintained because of repeated missed opportunities to ensure the existence of a properly constituted independent Board of Trustees. The latter is not the necessary and sufficient condition to ward off the five features of organisational inadequacy noted early in the chapter. However, it is a *necessary* condition.

Commentary from Pat Harvey

Previous chapters of this book describe aspects of their writers' frustrated efforts to engage in various aspects of the present-day functioning of the BPS in their capacities as long-term committed members. A detailed concluding analysis has been offered here by David Pilgrim. His approach has been typically scholarly. He has offered a succinct framework for conceptualising how and why the Society has arrived at its present juncture.

I believe that the BPS will pay no heed to this critique, or indeed the rest of this book. 'The BPS' does not constitute a coherent organisation that can form a Society-wide response or viewpoint, or recognise and respond dispassionately to crises or to differing analyses. It is now a large Society which has recently grown its fee-paying membership considerably, but most members are inactive and un-engaged. They may, for a number of reasons, be indifferent to, not just ignorant about, how the Society operates. After their initial flush of interest upon graduating or qualifying, most tend to dutifully to pay their fees and then record their membership for CV purposes.

With those members who actively seek to become engaged, the BPS has serious difficulties. The Korn Ferry Report, *Member Networks Review May 2021*, indicated that

> Member Networks identify a tension between corporate mind-set and the values they believe the Society should hold. Also, over-zealous compliance and control stifles productive activity, drains the energy and enthusiasm of Officers, and curtails and limits the autonomy people need to deliver the Society's Purpose effectively. This leads to huge amounts of frustration, disengagement, and ultimately the loss of Members' commitment (and potentially their membership).

Responses from members to posts on @psychsocwatchuk and BPSWatch.com have confirmed this picture. Overseeing the membership and the millions of pounds of income it provides, the BPS is a hydra-headed body of different leadership structures, salaried and voluntary. First, there is that of the CEO and the senior management team, most of whom are not psychologists. They have in recent years grown in number and become very evidently a career bureaucracy exercising autonomy and exerting control over other aspects of the structures (see Korn Ferry Report quotes above and below).

Second, the Board of Trustees, which should provide independent leadership oversight to the Society and to the bureaucratic structure and to which the CEO and SMT should be accountable, has proved incapable of so doing. It has completely lacked any true independence. Recent proposed changes will, in my view, make little real difference. Third, directly elected by the hitherto small proportion of members who exercise their vote, is the presidential team: president, vice president, and president-elect. Recent history has demonstrated how ineffectual this titular leadership function has been. In the full-scale crisis of 2021, reported below, their ineffectiveness took a darker turn.

In 2020, an extensive financial fraud had been discovered, carried out by the CEO's executive assistant. Astonishingly, this person, subsequently jailed in 2022, had been appointed despite previous criminal convictions for similar offences.[12] The Board of Trustees were belatedly to discover this was not the first significant financial irregularity in recent times but about which they had hitherto been kept in the dark. CEO and finance director were duly suspended in November 2020 to allow for an investigation to take place. The membership was not informed of the fact of this suspension. The suspended finance director moved on quickly to a post with the National Lottery Community Fund.

In 2021, there was to follow a catastrophic collapse of formal leadership at the BPS:

- The suspended CEO remained suspended, presumably on full salary, throughout most of 2021. The membership were finally told only when he returned in October 2021.[13] Although much of the fraudulent expenditure (shoes, cruise, hairdressing, underwear) was made on the CEO's card, and oversight of that expenditure had been inadequate or absent for months, the official BPS statement exonerated the CEO from any responsibility.
- The president, Dr Hazel McLoughlin, resigned in April 2021, for personal reasons.[14]

- The president-elect, Dr Nigel MacLennan, who had been success-ful in his election by members on an overtly reforming mandate, was expelled in May 2021, ostensibly for unspecified 'bullying'. The leadership then published a YouTube video, which was available for a time to the public, announcing this expulsion. This video was linked to on the open social media Twitter account of the former vice presi-dent, Dr David Murphy, until the link became inactive.[15]
- Vice president Dr David Murphy himself resigned in February 2021. He later published his full resignation letter on Twitter as a protest against what he saw as the incomplete and misleading report in *The Psychologist*. He stated that he had

> repeatedly raised concerns about aspects of the management of the Society and inadequacies in the oversight the board has pro-vided ... I have also persistently pressed for greater transparency and openness from the senior management team with trustees, members and BPS staff in the face of, what I believe to be, a dys-functional culture of secrecy and spin.

He refers to

> serious inadequacies in financial controls ... dramatically increasing recurrent expenditure of the Society over the past three years, almost all of which is accounted for by rising staff costs resulting from increases both in staff numbers and senior staff salaries ... significant reductions in many other areas of activity including member networks ... Society income has not kept pace with inflation over the last few years, yet staff costs have risen a staggering 73% just since 2018 and according to the now approved budget, in 2021 will be higher than the total income from basic membership and member networks combined.[16]

- These developments were reported in the national media during 2021: in *The Times*, *The Telegraph*, and *Third Sector* (see Chapter 3).
- During this period, it is believed that at least three psychologists resigned from the Board of Trustees.

Just prior to the events of 2021, in November 2020, the National Council for Voluntary Organisations (NCVO), which had been engaged by the BPS abruptly, and it turned out prophetically, withdrew from its contract when it discovered how toxic the climate that had evolved at the BPS had now become. It indicated that it did not wish to continue, as it feared that BPS staff and volunteers would suffer psychological and emotional harm, and that they would expose their own workers, who had requested to leave, to detriment. This alarming climate was reported in *Third Sector*:[17]

> We believe that continuing this work while the governance issues remain unresolved … would therefore be unethical. Given this, NCVO has a legal duty to protect its employees and associates and to ensure our consultants are not at risk. Members of our consultancy team felt the behaviours and culture affecting the leadership of BPS were detrimental to their wellbeing and requested to withdraw from the project … [highlighting] serious concerns from directors and trustees about the relationship between the senior management team and the board of trustees … [and that some staff and volunteers do not consider the charity] a safe or secure place for them.

In light of the above summary from the NCVO of the parlous state of the BPS culture, my personal view of the future of the organisation has changed since my active re-engagement with it occurred, coincidentally at the start of the Covid pandemic, and before the events of 2021 unfolded.

As a member for fifty years and a previous officeholder at the end of the 1990s, I came into the fray in 2020 because of specific disquieting matters concerning the recently published BPS guidelines on gender. Having then communicated with others, I came to understand, in a wider sense, how bad things had become. Structural contradictions and imbalances had become a stage-set for very evident cronyism amongst those volunteers who engage as long-term, sometimes self-styled, 'BPS junkies', and for policy capture by members who become activists for their 'causes' (see Chapters 4 and 5). However, my hope remained for some time that I might contribute to responsible pressures for real reform.

I no longer believe that the BPS can be rescued or reformed. It seems to me now that whatever governance reforms may be made, and however radical these may be, the Society will collapse under the weight of its own contradictions. Those inherent contradictions include the scientist/practitioner split, the ambiguous role of the Society in regulating psychology/psychologists, and the undermining impact of identity politics on properly considered policy-making. These problems are underpinned by the heterogonous pastiche which is the contemporary discipline of psychology and discussed by David Pilgrim here and in his earlier chapters.

It may be that, as David Pilgrim notes, the BPS may now fragment into sub-groups with clearer tribal identities, which offer direct respect and more relevance to their members, not reducing them to 'customers'. The emergence of organisations such as the ACP,[18] AEP,[19] and ABP[20] are symptoms of this fragmentation, and from hereon they may become the preferred choices of professional psychologists. Such contradictions may increasingly operate to undermine the perceived relevance of the Society to the bulk of its members.

The more direct route to the demise of the BPS may eventually all come down to money. The recent growth of membership has brought an enlarging revenue stream, but one that has encouraged the proliferation of a bureaucracy to bloating point. This has seen ever-increasing staffing levels and large executive salaries. As outlined above, this has occurred without a concomitant nurturing of member engagement. The old joke, 'This would be a great organisation if it weren't for the members', seems to be the attitude from the bureaucracy experienced by many in response to their representations. The resigning vice president sounded the alarm about this in the quotes given above. Similarly, the Korn Ferry exercise reported an evident disconnect between the centre of the BPS and its membership.

Taking a wider view of the structural context within which the BPS will be operating over the next decade, commercial expansion as a major means of survival may well be doomed. The BPS may have turned its efforts to expand its 'customer' base at its own ultimate expense. Climatic, economic, and societal shocks are likely to force rapid change upon the circumstances of the individuals who are members and potential members. This is likely to encourage their questioning of career-related benefits and affordability. Will a significant level of expenditure on membership of the BPS be seen as 'worth the money' to individual members with more stringent personal budgets?

A potentially stark decline of membership of professional bodies has been anticipated elsewhere, with warnings from consultancies worldwide who are offering their services to assist in 'future proofing' strategies.[21] The NCVO, before the withdrawal referred to above, had noted that the BPS had grown from a grassroots organisation to one of the biggest charities in the UK, and along the way its model of membership had evolved. It went on to suggest that, at 60,000 plus members, the models of decision-making that had served it in the past may not be the best fit for the future. Also, it noted how society is changing, and that the psychologists of the future may have different expectations of how the BPS should function. It suggested that the BPS needed to find models of power and decision-making that might work for it as a business. However, the important focus should be upon restoring and maintaining the confidence and engagement of its subscribing membership. That has not happened to date. Events from 2021 onwards suggest that, notwithstanding the serious concerns they had about BPS culture that precipitated their withdrawal, the NCVO formulation for change at the BPS was based upon an over-optimistic expectation of rational and honest organisational reflection.

I believe the evidence is that defensiveness, denial, and career self-interest has resolutely continued to drive the thinking and behaviour of the dominant regime. Indeed, the situation deteriorated further after Korn Ferry had warned that:

> Members said they felt as though 'the tail is wagging the dog': corporate procedures and governance that should help safeguard, connect and enable the organisation have become over-extended, driving the wrong organisational culture, procedures, and behaviours.

Changes in the wider context have also grown starker since the NCVO analysis was written in 2020. The NCVO may have underestimated in 2020 the extent to which membership in the sector they serve would be impacted in the medium-term future by economic shocks and their fall-out.

At this juncture, the controlling leadership of the BPS may well ignore this book, but as David Pilgrim put it in Chapter 7: 'The BPS provides an immediate and perfectly formed example of a dysfunctional organisation for students in management schools.' This is a deeply ironical fate for a Psychological Society that has failed to reflect, understand, or make real adjustments to its own dysfunction. What has happened is indeed a disquieting case study.

Notes

1. G. Bunn, A. D. Lovie, & G. D. Richards (2001). *Psychology in Britain: Historical Essays and Personal Reflections*. Leicester: BPS Books; J. Hall, D. Pilgrim, & G. Turpin (2015). *Clinical Psychology in Britain: Historical Perspectives*. Leicester: British Psychological Society.

2. H. W. Simons (1989). *Rhetoric in the Human Sciences*. London: Sage.

3. D. Pilgrim (2020). *Critical Realism for Psychologists*. London: Routledge.

4. P. Lencioni (2002). *The Five Dysfunctions of a Team*. New York: Jossey-Bass.

5. Y. Gamil, & I. A. Rahman (2017). Identification of causes and effects of poor communication in construction industry: A theoretical review. *Emerging Science Journal*, 1(4); C. C. Costinas (2012). Poor organizational communication, in *Annals of the West University of Timisoara*, Vol. VII (XXIV); K. Nagpal et al. (2010). A systematic quantitative assessment of risks associated with poor communication in surgical care. *Archives of* Surgery, 145(6): 582–588; D. Elder-Vass (2010). *The Causal Power of Social Structures: Emergence, Structure and Agency*. Cambridge: Cambridge University Press.

6. D. Stocker et al. (2010). Appreciation at work in the Swiss Armed Forces. *Swiss Journal of Psychology*, 69: 117–124.

7. C. L. Jurkiewicz, & R. A. Giacalone (2016). Organizational determinants of ethical dysfunctionality. *Journal of Business Ethics*, 136: 1–12; D. Shepherd (2016). *Complicit Silence: Organisations and Their Response to Occupational Fraud* (Doctoral dissertation, University of Portsmouth); F. Wettstein (2012). Silence as complicity: Elements of a corporate duty to speak out against the violation of human rights. *Business Ethics Quarterly*, 22(1): 37–61; T. M. Finser (2007). *Silence Is Complicity*. New York: Steiner Books; S. Dunne et al. (2008). Speaking out: The responsibilities of management intellectuals—A survey. *Organization*, 15(2): 271–282.

8. A. S. Cetinkaya, & S. Karayel (2019). The effects of organisational silence on work alienation in service enterprises. *International Journal of Economics and Business Research*, *18*(4): 480–498; R. Pope (2019). Organizational silence in the NHS: Hear no, see no, speak no. *Journal of Change Management*, *19*(1): 45–66; S. K. Pandey, & D. P. Moynihan (2005). Bureaucratic red tape and organizational performance: Testing the moderating role of culture and political support. *La Follette School Working Paper* No. 2005–026.

9. C. Cornforth (2005). *The Governance of Public and Non-Profit Organisations: What Do Boards Do?* London: Psychology Press; K. Ahmed et al. (2019). Organizational democracy and employee outcomes: The mediating role of organizational justice. *Business Strategy Development*, *2*: 204–219; A. Riege (2005). Three-dozen knowledge-sharing barriers managers must consider. *Journal of Knowledge Management*, *9*(3): 18–35; M. Mir et al. (2016). The impact of standardized innovation management systems on innovation capability and business performance: An empirical study. *Journal of Engineering and Technology Management*, *41*: 26–44; D. J. Campbell (2000). The proactive employee: Managing workplace initiative. *AMP*, *14*: 52–66.

10. The third edition of *A Sociology of Mental Health and Illness* (with Anne Rogers, Open University Press) was awarded first prize in the mental health category, and went on to win the all-category British Medical Association's Medical Book of the Year Award for 2006. At the time of writing, the book is in its sixth edition. Other publications of relevance to the BPS poverty group are: D. Pilgrim (2015). *Understanding Mental Health: A Critical Realist Exploration*. London: Routledge; A. Rogers, & D. Pilgrim (2003). *Mental Health and Inequality*. Basingstoke: Palgrave Macmillan; D. Pilgrim (2009). Mind the gender gap: Mental health in a post-feminist context. In: D. Kohen (Ed.), *Oxford Textbook of Women and Mental Health*. Oxford: Oxford University Press; D. Pilgrim (2008). The history of mental illness. In: K. Heggenhougen (Ed.), *Encyclopaedia of Public Health*. New York: Elsevier.

11. D. Pilgrim (2022). Verdicts on Eysenck and the fluxing context of British psychology. *History of the Human Sciences* (in press). https://doi.org/10.1177/09526951221143888

12. www.leicestermercury.co.uk/news/leicester-news/assistant-stole-more-70000-leicester-6470440

13. www.bps.org.uk/news-and-policy/statement-chief-executive-and-trustees-british-psychological-society

14. www.bps.org.uk/news-and-policy/bps-president-makes-%E2%80%98 difficult-decision%E2%80%99-step-down

15. https://twitter.com/ClinPsychDavid/status/1389632517079113734?s=20& t=ctPKFT7nohClqgZ3XVPnAQ

16. https://twitter.com/ClinPsychDavid/status/1394985946446184450?s=20& t=WHguWA43co2ZZbjs4lw0ag

17. www.thirdsector.co.uk/ncvo-pulled-consultancy-work-charity-amid-fears-detrimental-its-staff/management/article/1719976

18. https://acpuk.org.uk

19. https://www.aep.org.uk

20. https://theabp.org.uk

21. www.sidecarglobal.com/member-engagement/declining-membership-in-professional-organizations-and-what-you-can-do-about-it

CHAPTER 9

Some afterthoughts

D uring the writing of this book, a number of matters arose for the writers of the chapters. This afterword is an opportunity for the editor and two of the contributors to set out their final thoughts.

Graham Buchanan

Earlier, I discussed the notion of toxic leaders, but followers can have as much impact as any leader. Leaders and followers have a symbiotic relationship that needs to work effectively for the relationship to thrive. Both have expectations of the other, but for the relationship to work, the symbiosis must be mutualistic. In other words, both must benefit from the transaction.

For a leader to be successful, they must have people who are willing to follow their lead but, while followers can respect a leader's position, they don't necessarily have to respect the leader. Respect has to be earned.

Followers have expectations of their leaders which must be fulfilled before they will both respect them and, thus, willingly follow. Otherwise, their commitment will be, at best, grudging.

Every leader has a performance matrix they are measured against set by their employees, whether they know it or not. Failure to deliver against these expectations can turn the environment toxic, but strategies can be put in place to address followers' needs.

Research has shown that that followers have seven *critical* expectations of their leaders.

Followers expect:

1. 'Heroic leadership': Leaders who will 'take command' through crises to 'help us achieve the legitimate goals they have set'.

   They want leaders who don't hide away at the first sign of a crisis—people who are prepared to get stuck in alongside them.
2. 'Administrative leadership': Leaders who ensure that the logistics necessary for 'the success of their goals' are in place.

   There is little worse than being set a goal and then finding you don't have the resources to complete it.
3. 'Missionary leadership': Leaders who 'help us to grow and develop' to take on the mantle of future leadership, not in their mould, but in our own right.

   They want leaders to act as coaches and mentors, using their skill and experience to help people get on. What they don't want, however, is to become a clone or a puppet.
4. 'Creative leadership': Leaders who spell out a 'compelling proposition to take us with them on a journey into a foreseeable and successful future'.

   They will do what you ask, provided they know what it is, why they are doing it, and how they are to do it. They don't want some vague proposition that is bound to fail because nobody really understands it.
5. 'Optimistic leadership': Leaders who 'create an expectation of positive outcomes for the effort we put in; who make us believe and achieve'.

   They want a person who 'engenders hope', rather than cynicism and defeatism. But they also want that person to have the skill and will to help them achieve.
6. 'Caring leadership': Leaders who 'recognise our talent, acknowledge our achievements and are gentle with our rare failures'.

They want their 99 per cent of good work recognised over and above the 1 per cent of their work where they may have made a genuine mistake.

7. 'Candid leadership': Leaders who 'trust us enough to share both the good and the bad news, so we can work together towards achieving their compelling proposition'.

Followers are not stupid. They know when something is not right. While fully understanding that secrecy may, occasionally, be the order of the day, they really don't like being unnecessarily kept in the dark.

People follow effective leaders for many reasons, but followers' seven leadership expectations are fundamental and provide the basis for a successful leadership strategy.

'Toxic followers', on the other hand, are confused between the 'noble visions' of effective leaders and the 'grand illusions' of toxic leaders.

'Noble visions' set out a realistic view of the world that is achievable and of benefit to many other people, organisations, the environment, or just simply the world at large.

'Grand illusions' generate unrealistic dreams where eliminating any competition is the norm.

Remember, toxic leaders are self-serving and set themselves up as the 'saviour of the world' who we fail to follow at our peril, and they attract toxic followers, but they have no great love or compassion for them. If the follower fails, or questions, or challenges, they are dispensed with.

But the majority of followers are not *toxic*; they are conventional, and even though some of them may be hard work, they rarely become truly toxic.

The 10P follower model

All followers have a default position, but these roles are interchangeable with people moving readily from higher to lower levels if they believe the circumstances warrant it; and that is often as a result of poor leadership decisions.

The ten follower types are:

1. 'Proactive': 'the top 5 per cent'—prime movers; seek a 'new way'; and are conventionally ambitious (i.e., not toxic).

2. 'Positive': 'the next 90 per cent'—contribute well, adapting as the need arises. Good, steady performers who are the bulk of the organisation.

3. 'Player': will happily 'play the game' until something happens to move them into another, less positive, type if they don't get what they feel they deserve.

4. 'Pig': works well, but their snouts are permanently in the trough—their first consideration is 'WIIFM?' They won't do anything simply for the love of the job.

5. 'Passive': so anonymous people ask, 'Who is that?' That is, until they are pushed to their limit—then watch out.

6. 'Pessimist': 'We're all doomed', but few people listen. Occasionally they get it right, which merely reinforces their worldview.

7. 'Passenger': here in body, but not in mind. Totally uncommitted.

8. 'Prisoner': competent—in a rut and wants to leave, but they have nowhere to go—in any event, who would have them?

9. 'Provocateur': deliberately controversial to provoke argument or other strong reactions which can, occasionally, be useful, but often the provocation is unwarranted.

10. 'Poisoner': 'the 0.1 per cent' whose sole aim is to poison every part of the organisation, irrespective of who they harm or the damage they do. They don't just want to rock the boat, they want to destroy it. These are not toxic followers; these people are often bitter for some reason that is not clear. They view all leaders as 'toxic' because they cannot meet their extortionate needs.

While everybody has a default position, anybody can adopt any position as the mood takes them. They can wear them like a coat, pulling them on and off as they like.

Ashley Conway

I have had a long-term interest in the dogma of 'false memory syndrome' (FMS) and its advocates. I am not particularly surprised that there are some people who believe in this, despite its lack of scientific plausibility. I am, though, surprised that this group of believers includes a small number of psychologists. More surprising still, I find it very strange that a professional society like the BPS should produce policy documents that seem to be inappropriately influenced by the FMS rhetoric—despite the overwhelming evidence that their story is unscientific and harmful to victims of abuse.

I began to search for an explanation of how this happened within the BPS. I looked at the committees producing policy documents that seem to be sympathetic to the FMS line. I then tried to understand how these committees were chosen (and occasionally shut down, having no documentation to show for their work). This was a bizarrely difficult task. The formation and closure of one of the groups (2013) seems to be almost a secret to this day. Finding myself deeply frustrated, I eventually discovered from colleagues in other specialties that my problem was far from unique, and indeed was possibly the norm. BPS policy was being determined by groups of people where there was no visible due process in terms of selection of membership of a committee, no clarity about who determined terms of reference, and no clear oversight of the process of the functioning and conclusions of these groups.

Having failed to get answers to my questions through any normal route, I decided to go to the trustees, who have the ultimate responsibility for governance. Then I discovered that a number of the trustees were the very people about whom I was wanting to ask questions. The BPS is a charity, and the Charity Commission has rules and guidelines, including that trustees should have no conflicts of interest. Yet in the BPS, it is the norm for trustees to have two or more roles, with the potential (almost inevitability) for such conflicts to be significant.

As I learned more (principally through BPSWatch.com), I discovered that these conflicts of interest ran wide and deep, into virtually every area of function of the Society. Apart from the FMS policy, there were others that were controversial—for example, policy relating to gender identity. Also, there were massive question marks about procurement and oversight of large budget expenses, such as the £6 million for a 'Change Programme', with little or no transparency about where money has gone or what was to show for it. There was a huge fraud which was not explained to members, and there had been an arson attack at the BPS head offices unreported to members.

At the time of writing, there have been statements, repeated by the BPS on social media, that the Society is alienating itself from Russian psychologists because of Putin's invasion of Ukraine. 'Today, we have voted to support the expulsion of Russia from the European Federation of Psychologists' Association as a demonstration of our solidarity with Ukraine.' Note the use of the word 'we' here, without any explanation of who 'we' are or who in the BPS decided to post these tweets. The response on Twitter was almost universally negative: 'Not a show of solidarity, but punishment of a group on grounds of national origin (Prejudice)'; 'Such a big decision should not be taken without consulting members'; 'Collective guilt and collective punishment from a society that has the word psychology in their name, Unbelievable'; 'Wow, have no words … This is discrimination'; 'Politically impartial as ever then?'

In early 2022, the BPS organised a restructuring which required a vote of approval from members. The trustees voted to retain themselves. The BPS lobbied members heavily to vote 'yes' to their proposals. Such is the apathy among members that less than 10 per cent voted. Less than 8 per cent of the electorate voted 'yes' as recommended by the Society, but this was enough for them to bring in sweeping changes. Unfortunately, the sweeping changes look like they are going to be for the worse. Conflicts of interest remain. In a tweet thread, David Murphy, an ex-BPS president and chair of the group overseeing the changes, and trustee for six years, opined:

> There are so many changes that I find them quite hard to follow myself … some are great, but others would be a disaster … The new proposal is for 2/3rds of the Board of Trustees to be appointed by … the Board itself, not elected by anyone … There is no explanation provided for many new Trustee powers … including power to lend money and give credit to … any person or company … I believe the BPS needs MORE accountability and transparency not LESS … I will therefore be voting AGAINST.

What is needed, given the above picture of inadequate democratic accountability? My belief is that the BPS needs a radical overhaul of the structure of the Board of Trustees. The Board has now become less democratic, and in conflict with Charity Commission guidance, it will continue to contain numerous members with a conflict of interest. Governance is supposedly the responsibility of the trustees. However, for now, the person with the title 'head of legal and governance' is *not* a trustee. The BPS website tells us that access to the BoT is via the CEO. How does that work? What if the CEO or 'head of governance' does not want an issue raised with the Board? Again, according to the BPS website, the Board of Trustees is:

> the Society's primary governing body, with responsibility for the management and control of the Society's affairs and transactions, which ensures that we conform to the terms of our charter and that we observe our legal obligations as a charitable body.

The trustees are supposed to be ultimately responsible for position statements and governance. Over many years, they have failed in these vital tasks because the Board is not fit for purpose. As a consequence, the BPS is a failed charitable organisation. The system of governance needs a complete overhaul, probably imposed from an outside agency, as the BPS seems incapable of doing this itself.

David Pilgrim

Editing this book has been challenging for a number of reasons. The most important one has been the dilemma for all the contributors of an elephant in the room. Those who have observed the shenanigans at the centre of the BPS, in recent years, will have noted that reforming presidents have been given short shrift by those with power and under threat. In her commentary on my final chapter, Pat Harvey made a passing allusion to the expulsion of Nigel MacLennan. In my view, this was a significant event in more ways than one. Others, such as recent past presidents Peter Kinderman and Jamie Hacker-Hughes, were dealt with harshly by the Board of Trustees. However, the most draconian measure of expulsion was reserved for MacLennan.

Above, Ashley Conway also reminds us that another president, David Murphy, who became frustrated with what he encountered about basic expectations of good governance, resigned before his term of office was up. We can only speculate about how he may have been treated, had he remained in office and recorded his grave concerns publicly, instead of broadcasting his resignation letter on social media.

The contributors to this book are highly familiar with this cultural norm, within the BPS, of punishment instinctively being meted out to critics. As we have found out recurrently, critics are ignored, and if they cannot be ignored, they are punished. However, the MacLennan case stands out because of its gravity, in relation to both natural justice and democracy. We have all been constrained by anxieties about *sub judice* and have erred on the side of caution about expressing both what we know and our value judgements about it. The law scares people; it was used, for a while successfully, by the leadership of the BPS to intimidate us about our activity on BPSWatch.

Sub judice is a particularly difficult matter to anticipate and respect properly, mainly because there are no black and white rules laid out in advance to guide anyone (lawyers or the public). If a claim or statement is ever designated to fall foul of *sub judice*, it is only a *post hoc* judgement in a particular case. In other words, anyone only knows that they have 'got it wrong' (i.e., by demonstrably prejudicing a criminal or civil legal proceeding) after the event.

In my view, there is more than a whiff of absurdity about this constraint on freedom of expression, especially when a commentator is offering a serious view in good faith, with reference to facts already in the public domain and aimed at serving the public interest. In order to demystify the reader as much as is reasonably possible, within this dilemma in this particular case, I can say this much because they are material facts already in the public domain and on record.

First, MacLennan made his critical views about the governance of the BPS very clear in his candidate statement, when offering to serve as president of the BPS. Second, he was elected legitimately on that platform. Third, he was accused of bullying a member of BPS staff. Fourth, he was expelled by the Board of Trustees, announced very publicly, using a YouTube posting. Fifth, that posting was made in advance of him being allowed to appeal the decision. Sixth, an appeal was then heard, and the invited panel chosen by the Board of Trustees then confirmed the expulsion. Seventh, Nigel MacLennan was expelled as both a BPS member and its president. Eighth, the Board of Trustees then permitted an election for his temporary replacement but broke with election convention for the first time on record. The candidates for the replacement were not allowed to be drawn from the general membership (the norm under rule) but instead only senate members or trustees could be candidates. Ninth, MacLennan took his grievance, about the facts surrounding the above, to the employment tribunal system, and his case is due to be heard presently.

Generally, as the name implies, an employment tribunal is a court reserved to consider cases of legally aggrieved employees. However, the MacLennan case follows a recent precedent, when a case was heard about a non-employee. This is politically important, given that senior leaders in any organisation may be elected or appointed. That is, they are not employed but they act in their role, instead, in a voluntary capacity. That was the case with MacLennan, and so the tribunal system is treating him on this occasion as a *de facto* employee governed by legal expectations.

The full story of this case, and its implications for matters discussed in the chapters of this book, about the culture of the BPS, will become clear after the tribunal has made its decision. Apart from the judgement from the tribunal and MacLennan's account afterwards, it is likely that the public will have access to its implications for the BPS, as well as its current and past leaders, from reports in the mass media.

Watch this space.

Index